INTERPRETING THE GOSPELS
FOR PREACHING

D. MOODY SMITH

Interpreting
the Gospels
for Preaching

FORTRESS PRESS   PHILADELPHIA

Library of Congress Cataloging in Publication Data

Smith, Dwight Moody.
   Interpreting the Gospels for preaching.

   Bibliography: p.
   Includes index.
   1. Bible. N.T. Gospels—Homiletical use—Addresses, essays, lectures. I. Title.
BS2555.4.S6   251   79–8900
ISBN 0–8006–1381–3

8018J79   Printed in the United States of America   1–1381

In Memory of James T. Cleland
1903–1978
A Servant of the True and Lively Word

CONTENTS

Preface   ix

Part One: Gospel Criticism and Exegesis for Preaching

1. Preaching from the Gospels: The Historical Question   3

2. The Gospels as the Church's Preaching: Form Criticism   15

3. The Gospels as the Evangelists' Preaching:
   Redaction Criticism   29

Part Two: Preaching from the Synoptic Gospels:
            Some Paradigms and Specimens

4. Preaching from Mark   45

5. Preaching from Matthew   55

6. Preaching from Luke   66

Part Three: Preaching from the Gospel of John:
             A Different but Related Task

7. The Character of the Fourth Gospel   79

8. The Exegesis of the Fourth Gospel:
   Jesus' Farewell (John 16)   83

9. Problems and Perspectives in Preaching
   from John and the Synoptics   95

Conclusion   103

Notes   105

Bibliography   111

Indexes   113

PREFACE

JAMES T. CLELAND, late Dean of Duke Chapel and James B. Duke Professor of Preaching in the Divinity School, made all his students aware of the basic problematic of preaching, namely, the exposition of the word of God on the basis of Scripture in ever-changing human situations. To speak in the spirit if not the words of Cleland, this means preaching from where the text is to where the people are. Or, perhaps better put, it is preaching from where the church was to where the church is. However that may be, exegesis, interpretation that is historically defensible, is demanded.

Because this small book owes something significant by way of inspiration, and whatever insight it may contain, to Cleland, who taught me the indispensable connection between exegesis and preaching, it is appropriately dedicated to his memory. The book is not about preaching per se or about the Gospels per se, but about the nexus between them. I readily acknowledge that effective Christian preaching demands more—although not less—than exegetical skill and insight. There is no attempt to define preaching or to contribute to its development as a discipline, except insofar as the discussion of preaching from the Gospels may contribute to such definition and development. I am aware, although certainly not master, of the growing body of literature in that field. Nor do I deal with questions of gospel criticism or even interpretation except as they may contribute to understanding and accomplishing the work of preaching. I have in general adopted the position of widest consensus on questions of New Testament scholarship. This means, for example, that the Marcan, or two-document, hypothesis is accepted, as well as the basic insights and perspectives—although not all the varied and in some respects contradictory results—of form and redaction criticism.

Much of what I say may have a familiar ring. I have endeavored to show the relevance for preaching of the insights gained through the biblical scholarship of the past half-century or more. Some new pathways of literary criticism and structuralism that have opened up within

the last decade are left unexplored here. If the work seems therefore to
be old stuff to the readers, well and good. Let them leave it on one side
and go on to other things. But the kinds of considerations presented here
are in my judgment necessary, important, and potentially quite helpful
for preaching. Such historically oriented questions are not optional, but
germane to Christian interpretation. In much of the preaching we hear
today these questions are not taken into account, and it therefore
seemed worthwhile to call attention to them in this way. With some fear
and trembling I present a couple of examples from my own preaching,
not so much as criteria but as stimulus for further discussion.

Several chapters of the book were delivered in similar form as lectures
to theological students at Duke, at the 1979 Pastors' Convocation of the
Virginia Conference of the United Methodist Church, and to a small but
critically appreciative group of ministers attending the Continuing Edu-
cation Seminars of Duke Divinity School in the same year. Portions of
Part Three were published in my book on *John* in the Proclamation
Commentaries series and are reprinted with permission of the pub-
lisher. The sermon on the Lucan Annunciation and part of the discussion concerning it are used with the kind permission of the publishers of
Interpretation: A Journal of Bible and Theology. Material excerpted
from *The Secret of Happiness* by Billy Graham, copyright © 1955 by
Billy Graham, has been reprinted by permission of Doubleday & Company Inc., and World's Work, Ltd. Quotations from *The Jesus of
History* by T. R. Glover are used by permission of Association Press. My
colleagues Richard Lischer, William H. Willimon, and Franklin W.
Young of Duke Divinity School read the manuscript and offered encouragement and suggestions. I am grateful to them. Naturally the
author alone must bear responsibility for the book's contents.

D. MOODY SMITH

PART ONE

Gospel Criticism
and Exégesis for Preaching

1

PREACHING FROM THE GOSPELS:
THE HISTORICAL QUESTION

BEFORE PREACHING from the Gospels the interpreter needs to ask seriously what they are. This question may best be put after first considering briefly what the Bible as a whole is. The Gospels will then be found to be examples of a broader species.

It may be trite, but it is nevertheless true, to say that the Bible is the church's book in that it contains the testimony of the people of God, shaped by the people of God, preserved by and for the people of God. To affirm this is to utter a theological as well as a sociological and historical truth.

The faith of the Christian church is not faith in a book, but it is nourished by the belief that in this book is found indispensable testimony to the Word of God and that from this book the Word of God ever and again finds human shape and voice. The book has its origin and life within the community of faith and thus speaks from faith for faith (Rom. 1:17). Wherever the message of that book was first grasped and appropriated as such, there was the people of God—in the sense in which the biblical writers use that and similar terms. Wherever that message is grasped and appropriated, that same people of God appears. Ingredient to this proposition is the belief, indeed faith, that there is *a* message, as opposed to many messages or no message, and that this message can be heard and owned, appropriated, in situations far removed from its inception. Thus it involves the belief, tacit or implicit, that there exists a real and significant identity and continuity between the originative community or communities of the biblical word and the many communities in which it was and continues to be read and heard. Perhaps the principal means of establishing and articulating that continuity is preaching.

At the level of sociological description rather than theological assertion it is also correct to say that the Scriptures are the churches' (not
church's) book. Here the definition of the religious communities needs
to be broadened to include synagogues, at least as far as the Old
Testament is concerned. Historical exegesis and study that make no
theological claims can scarcely justify the assertion that there is a
message, or one message, of Scripture, or one church spanning two (or
three) thousand years. Yet even at this level it is manifestly the case that
the Bible is the product of the religious communities that produced and
preserved it. Moreover, it continues to be used in churches (or
synagogues) which at least claim a direct connection, and even identity,
with the originative communities. Thus, at this level too it is not
meaningless to claim that the Bible is the churches' book. There was
never a Bible apart from the church. While there was a church apart
from the Bible, it did not exist prior to or apart from the reality to which
the Bible witnesses. What is more, wherever the Bible is looked to as
the source or ground of religious community, there is preaching in
some form.

All this has been said before and in much greater detail. Nevertheless,
in any consideration of preaching from the Gospels it is necessary to
recall and reiterate the churchly, community origins, as well as use, of
the Bible as a whole. When that is said, however, we must also make
clear to ourselves what is *not* meant. To say that the Bible is the
church's book does not mean that the church (or churches) tells the
Bible what to say, that the institutional church is the sole arbiter of the
biblical message.

In Protestant churches it has been acknowledged in theory, if not
always in fact, that the authority of Scripture stands over against the
church as a norm to which the church must conform. The importance
that preaching has in the Protestant tradition attests to this conviction.
Yet even here, indeed sometimes most of all here, the church has
presumed to tell the Bible what to say—never, or almost never, con-
sciously, but in the assumptions that have undergirded exegesis. From
our perspective the most obvious examples are found in the rationalism
of the eighteenth century and the theological liberalism of the nineteenth century. Albert Schweitzer showed convincingly how the assumptions of a Western, liberal mentality had determined allegedly
historical portrayals of Jesus of Nazareth so that the radical, es-

chatological character of his message was not allowed to appear;[1] God's word had been identified with the truths of reason or with the values of enlightened liberalism or with a certain kind of pietism, and modern portrayals of Jesus conformed to the pattern set. One might well ask how much the preaching in today's liberal and so-called main-line American churches still owes to such assumptions and allegiances.

But it is not from that side alone that words are still being put into the Bible's mouth. Much that has gone under the banners of conservative, biblical, evangelical, or fundamentalist preaching is predicated on assumptions different from or foreign to the Bible. One thinks especially of the narrowly individualistic, spiritualistic, and pietistic assumptions that govern much preaching of this sort. It is assumed that the Bible speaks only to individual needs and salvation. It is assumed that salvation refers only to the state of the individual after death. It is assumed that Scripture teaches total abstinence from alcoholic beverages and other tabooed behavior. None of these assumptions is justified, although each is widespread. (A most significant development in some American conservative and evangelical circles today is the abandonment of such assumptions and the recognition that the Bible, or God through the Bible, may have something to say to the corporate or social condition of humanity here and now.)

The point need not be belabored. Whether with the best or the worst of intentions and motivations, Christians, especially those who preach, have put their own words into the Bible's mouth. There may be a sense in which, or an extent to which, this is inevitable. In appropriating the Bible we must make it our own. In making it our own, there is the danger that we will confuse its message with our own. The risk must be taken; the danger is unavoidable. What we must continually ask ourselves is how the danger can be guarded against or minimized.

The danger or temptation to make the Bible say what we want it to say is perhaps greatest in the Gospels. There we are closest to the heart of most Christian belief and piety. Christians who read the Gospels and preachers who preach from them rightly feel that in so doing they are coming close to Jesus himself. In the Gospels the reader or preacher is presented with portrayals of Jesus, and it may reasonably be claimed that in these portrayals one is in a real sense confronted with him. But it is perhaps precisely here that the danger of misleading misinterpretation is greatest, for at the point of the Gospels' presentation and interpretation of Jesus and the reader's or hearer's understanding and appropriation of it, so much is at stake.

Moreover, we are too prone to assume that Jesus really is the guardian of all that we count dearest. Since the dawn of modernism and the attempt to free the real, historical Jesus from the encrustation of church dogma, there have been numerous attempts to claim Jesus for worthwhile human causes. Most recently, and with some justification, Jesus has appeared as the liberator of blacks, of women, of the poor and oppressed minorities. At the same time denizens of country clubs and chambers of commerce, not to mention the lodges and union halls, continue to assume that Jesus undergirds their dearest values. Archie Bunker never doubts that his concept of what is right and proper coincides with the Lord's.

Almost all of us, Christians and many non-Christians, would like to enlist Jesus in our cause, or even to enlist in the cause of Jesus. Paul, by contrast, is not so popular. Indeed, Paul has been regarded, even by some Christians, as expendable if not downright deplorable. Some black Christians have found Paul's alleged tolerance of the status quo reprehensible, while some feminist Christians believe Paul's assertion that in Christ there is neither male nor female is less heartfelt than his efforts to maintain women in what he regarded as their suitable and proper place. Most of us have probably continued to assume that Paul was a less attractive person than Jesus, although there is little hard evidence to support that assumption. The picture of Paul as a short, bald-headed, bowlegged Jew is in all probability legendary rather than historical, and it may owe something to anti-Semitism.[2] The picture of Jesus as tall and fair, not to say blond, with an aquiline nose owes as much or more to Sallman's *Head of Christ* and other Sunday school art as to the New Testament.

But the only Jesus we have comes to us through the pages of the New Testament, and the only authorized portrayals of his humanity appear in four canonical Gospels. That there may be genuine sayings of Jesus in apocryphal books and other literature need not be denied. Acts, the Epistles, and Revelation also convey a palpable sense of who or what Jesus was like. Yet we read the latter in the light of what we find in the New Testament Gospels, and we must guard against the too easy assumption that they all presuppose the Gospels' portrayals. They do not, although there is a real question as to whether we can finally make sense of them apart from the Gospels.

It is perhaps a characteristic of American Protestant theology and piety to assume that the Gospels and the historical Jesus behind the Gospels are central to any understanding of Christian faith and practice. Something of the heritage of liberal theology, as well as the ancient theology that informed the shape of the canon, may live on here. On the other hand, one has to acknowledge that some Christians, even and especially in the evangelical tradition, have found the pivotal point in Paul, and particularly in the Epistle to the Romans. Others have found it, among the Gospels, in John, which has frequently been accounted by modern critical scholarship the least historical of the four. One should not, therefore, too easily take for granted the centrality of the Gospels, especially the Gospels' witness to the historical Jesus, as the New Testament basis for Christian faith. It is by no means certain that the memory of the historical Jesus dominated and determined all the earliest Christian preaching. (The obverse, that it had virtually nothing to do with it, is also subject to serious question.) There is no need, however, to disparage or play down the role of Jesus. The dominant place of the Gospels in the canon testifies to that. But one must at the same time be aware of the dangers and difficulties in attempting to recover and appropriate Jesus. In what follows I want to suggest how and in what sense Christianity's rootage in the mission and message of Jesus may be responsibly brought to expression in preaching.

In my own conviction, that rootage in Jesus cannot be adequately expressed apart from the Gospels. Certainly in the church it cannot be adequately expressed apart from preaching from the Gospels. To preach the gospel adequately and fully one must preach from the Gospels, but to preach from the Gospels we must understand and appreciate what they are. They are based upon the gospel message. It is no exaggeration to say that we are now in a better position than our immediate predecessors to understand and appreciate the Gospels and to preach the gospel from them. (Certainly one should not think that the gospel has not been preached from the Gospels in earlier periods, but the deficiencies or inadequacies of earlier generations do not excuse us from making our best efforts!) To understand the Gospels means, first of all, to recognize that they are not historical by modern standards of historical writing. To assume that they are is a mistake that easily leads to misunderstanding them and therefore preaching from them in misleading ways.

What it means to misunderstand the Gospels and therefore to preach from them in misleading ways can best be illustrated by an example from the history of gospel criticism and interpretation. As we have noted, Albert Schweitzer (in his justly renowed *The Quest of the Historical Jesus* [1906; English translation 1910]) wrote the history and the obituary of the liberal efforts to present the life of Jesus and to erect edifices of theology and even faith upon it. Yet in 1917, as if Schweitzer had never lived or written, the Cambridge University classical historian T. R. Glover published a short book entitled *The Jesus of History*. Glover's book is not important in the history of biblical scholarship, but it is important for our purposes because it represents a view of Jesus and of the Gospels that is typical of modern scholarship before Schweitzer and is still very much alive in preaching and piety today. Even as today's lay theology is the, perhaps attenuated, product of yesteryear's academic theology, so today's popular exegesis and preaching is the product of yesteryear's biblical scholarship, misguided though it may have been. My secondhand copy of Glover, helpfully underlined and annotated, once belonged to a Methodist minister in Ohio, who had apparently used it in a college or seminary course. In this copy it is easy to find those statements that are typical of the whole liberal biographical view of Jesus and the Gospels—statements that are most dubious or questionable today—because they have been carefully underlined by the previous owner of the book. Furthermore, the work bears explicit or implicit churchly imprimaturs. There is a foreword by the archbishop of Canterbury, dated Advent Sunday 1916. The book was published by the Student Christian Movement in Great Britain and by Association Press in this country.

The conviction and presupposition of Glover's work is that Christian faith, if it is not dependent upon historical knowledge of Jesus, will be vastly deepened and enriched by it. Such knowledge can easily be gleaned from the Gospels, at least from the synoptics, if they are subjected to the careful scrutiny of the modern historian. "If one thing more than another marks modern thought," writes Glover in the first sentence of the book, "it is a new insistence on fact." On the basis of the Gospel accounts he proceeds to lay out the "facts" about Jesus, with a robust confidence in their power to convince and convict. The belief that the Gospels are *historical documents* undergirds and informs Glover's work from beginning to end, even though he recognizes that they are not biographies in the proper sense of the term. Yet, "we may be secure in using them as genuine and untouched reproductions of what he said and thought."[3]

At two crucial points in Glover's work the collision is clear between Schweitzer's powerfully articulated case against conventional modern pictures of Jesus and Glover's typically liberal assumptions, governed as they are by an interest in historical reconstruction. In the first place, Glover draws inferences from the Gospels about Jesus' intentions and personal relationships where there is little, or at least no unambiguous, warrant in the text for doing so. Thus he supplies an extraneous key or framework for their interpretation. One example of this method and its results will suffice. Glover writes, "The Gospel began with friendship, and we know from common life what that is, and how it works." He then proceeds to describe how friendship (that is, the friendship of Jesus and his disciples) begins and grows:

> Pleasant and easy-going, a perpetual source of interest and rest of mind, the friendship continues, till we find to our surprise that we are changed. Stage by stage, as one comes to know one's friend, by unconscious and freely given sympathy, one lives the other man's life, sees and feels things as he does, slips into his language, and, by degrees, into his thoughts—and then wakes up to find oneself, as it were, remade by the other's personality, so close has been the identification with the man we grew to love. This is what we find in our own lives; and we find it in the Gospels.[4]

Here is a classic and beautiful example of Gospel interpretation between the lines. The author, without realizing it, supplies an interpretive framework for the Gospel's portrayal of Jesus and his followers. The interpretation is based on a piety and imagination whose source is somewhere or something other than the Gospels. The picture Glover paints fits the relationship of Socrates and his disciples as described in the dialogues of Plato better than it does the relationship of Jesus and his disciples as described in the canonical Gospels. And it does not fit the impact the Gospel writers apparently intended their books to have on us as Christian, or interested, readers. In the Gospels the disciples do not understand Jesus better the longer they stay with him; they do not grow as their personalities are suffused by his. Rather, it would be more accurate to say that the longer they were with him the less they understood him, until at last one betrayed him, their leader denied him, and they all fled.

Such speculative—actually fictional—interpretation of Jesus is frequently found in preaching, and often as here in connection with Jesus' personal relationships, whether with his disciples or with others. The story of the so-called Rich Young Ruler (Mark 10:17–22) affords an example of this sort of imaginative eisegesis (that is, leading a meaning into the text):

> Jesus was drawn to this youth, I suspect, not so much for what he was as what he might become. He saw in him possibilities which the man did not know he had—possibilities of courage, kindness, daring, self-sacrifice. Just as Jesus saw rocklike strength and endurance hidden in impulsive Peter; saw loyal discipleship lurking in office-seeking James and John; saw a possible Christian leader in Zacchaeus, who had been no more than a fat official; saw promise of sainthood in Mary Magdalene; so here.[5]

Or again:

> A crowd of people is listening to Jesus at Capernaum. On the outskirts of the crowd is a man past middle age, whose face we can tenderly read.
>   You notice the lines under his eyes. You notice that he drops his eyes if anyone looks keenly at him. You notice that the corners of his mouth run down and that there are heavy lines there too. You notice his stooping figure and shuffling gait as he walks homeward as the crowd breaks up. You catch the gleam of tears in his eyes. His heart is heavy. He is a despised tax gatherer. His name is Matthew, a despicable name.
>   But when he listened to Jesus something that was still splendid and not quite dead in him fluttered within his breast. And as he is going home he is saying to himself, "Ah, it is very beautiful and I should like to be like that, but I am not. The tracks of habit are too deep. And how should I get my living and what would people say?"

But later:

> A shadow fell across Matthew's ledger onto a page on which but recently the tears of a man growing old made the ink run. And Matthew looked up into those eyes that are the homes of all men's dreams; and looking into the face of Jesus he realized in a flash two things, that Jesus believed in him, and that Jesus knew best what was holding him back.[6]

Such words may be ennobling or evocative of fine pious sentiments; the descriptions may even be true in the way that imaginative scenes in a historical novel may have the ring of authenticity about them. However that may be, these descriptive scenes have little or no basis in the

Gospels. They represent wholesale fabrication based on psychological speculation. Whether such fabrications are good or bad, harmful or helpful, may be debatable. Nevertheless, it is the task of theologically responsible exegesis to call attention to what they are.

Glover collides with Schweitzer, in the second place, in that despite Glover's maxim "to give the man's words his own meaning" he has very little to say about Jesus' preaching of the kingdom of God, and what is said plays down its eschatological character and ignores its apocalyptic background.[7] Correctly noting that Jesus himself does not analyze or explain what he means by kingdom of God or kingdom of heaven, Glover briefly considers the possibility of interpreting the concept against its contemporary Jewish background, presumably apocalyptic. This possibility he dismisses, however, with the observation that "it is always bad criticism to give to the words of genius the value or the connotation they would have on the lips of ordinary people." Not a bad insight, but apparently it is the rationale for a tacit but nevertheless unjustifiable dismissal of the possible, indeed probable, apocalyptic background of Jesus' use of the concept. Jesus' urgent message that the kingdom is at hand is replaced in Glover's presentation by a general and vague orientation toward the future.

A similar neglect of the eschatological character of Jesus' message is also characteristic of much preaching, even in sermons where it might well be emphasized. Billy Graham's book on Jesus' teaching about happiness is in effect a series of sermons—the style is unmistakably homiletical—on the Beatitudes.[8] One is struck by the fact that the treatment of the first beatitude, "Blessed are the poor in spirit, for theirs is the kingdom of heaven," is a rather moralistic homily on the nature and virtue of spiritual poverty.[9] Virtually nothing is said about the kingdom of heaven, although the term appears in the text. The modern preacher, like Jesus himself, seems to assume that the hearer will understand what is meant. But their respective hearers will surely not have the same understanding of that term. The question of the meaning and relevance of Jesus' proclamation of the kingdom is a real and difficult one, as New Testament study and theology have taught us. But it is not only in those academic circles in which the problem has been most sharply focused that Jesus' message of the kingdom has been ignored. The modern evangelist also seems to ignore it and treats this beatitude, like the others, as a prescription for happiness or for the ills of human-

kind. Moreover, he too indulges in the kind of imaginative construc-
tions we have already observed as he describes the setting of the Sermon
on the Mount:

> The air is tense. It is a moment to be captured and held for eternity. The
> crowd hushes as Jesus climbs atop a large red rock and is seated. In the
> valley on the desert road, a lone camel rider winds his way along the trail to
> Tiberias. A quiet falls upon the multitude as their faces gaze expectantly at
> Jesus. Then he opens his mouth and begins to speak.[10]

Whether Albert Schweitzer arrived at an adequate mode and method
for understanding the Gospels and appropriating their message about
Jesus remains a real question. Probably he did not. The abiding merit of
Schweitzer's work, however, is that he put his finger upon those factors
that were vitiating a proper historical, literary, and theological understanding of the Gospels. Jesus was being domesticated by a refusal to
recognize his strangeness, especially his eschatology, and by an imposi-
tion upon the Gospels of hermeneutical or interpretive conceptions and
assumptions that are congenial to us but foreign to the New Testament—for example, the concept of Jesus' developing relationship of
friendship with his disciples.

Schweitzer's work has had a profound effect upon New Testament
scholarship and upon the teaching of New Testament in universities and
seminaries. It has had much less effect on the preaching and teaching of
the churches. The Jesus I learned about in Sunday school and church,
fully a generation after Schweitzer, was the Jesus of T. R. Glover. But
what saint was constantly held up as an example of Christian discipleship, following Jesus? Albert Schweitzer, of course. We were told
everything about Schweitzer except what he really believed about Jesus!
Incidentally, the mission board under whose auspices Schweitzer first
went to Africa forbade him to preach to the people. Thus the natives of
the Congo like the natives of my home church were held in ignorance of
Schweitzer's radical beliefs. I had a mental image of Schweitzer following the friendly Jesus of Glover off to Africa to make friends with and
help the people there.

Perhaps I am being too harsh. The Jesus of Schweitzer was a problematic figure, historically as well as theologically, but after Schweitzer
the Jesus of Glover is an impossibility for the intellectually responsible
reader of the Gospel. But what about the preacher? There is a sense in
which the preacher has been deprived of a relationship to Jesus, particu-

larly the friendly and easily accessible Jesus, which he can claim and commend. He seems to have lost a great deal. But again I think of my own personal experience. I found that particular Jesus attractive but not compelling. In my childhood and youth one question kept coming back to me: Why that Jesus at all? I had friends. I believed in God. Or, more truthfully, I was concerned about faith in God. But nobody tried to explain to me exactly what Jesus had to do with faith in God or with any of the other fundamental questions I was asking at that time. Perhaps it is not so surprising that in the long run this attractive, friendly, accessible Jesus has not attracted a large or permanent following. I believe it can be shown that the church has grown flaccid and, ultimately, smaller where this Jesus has been preached.

Fortunately, in the final analysis, we are not stuck with a choice between Schweitzer's Jesus and Glover's Jesus. Important developments in the analysis and interpretation of the Gospels have occurred in the intervening years. Some of these have, I think quite wrongly, been viewed as destructive to faith and therefore detrimental to preaching, but I find them liberating and enabling for faith and very fruitful for preaching. To these we shall now turn.

2

THE GOSPELS AS THE
CHURCH'S PREACHING:
FORM CRITICISM

FORM CRITICISM as a discipline or method of biblical scholarship was developed in Germany, where it is known as *Formgeschichte* (form history). That name is more adequate than its customary English counterpart, for it makes clear that more is at stake than mere literary or traditional form. Form criticism is the study of the individual units of tradition—sayings, stories, parables, apocalyptic discourses—with a view to understanding how their form is related to their function and history in the primitive church. Form critics assume that most of the tradition originally existed as individual units and that there was a stage at which these units of tradition, stories and sayings, were told and retold by word of mouth (cf. 1 Cor. 11:23); they assume that such traditional units were preserved and transmitted because they served a need and purpose in the church. Form criticism has proved credible insofar as it has been able to postulate settings, functions, and histories for units of tradition which shed light upon their meaning and interpretation. Because form criticism deals with the earliest church setting of the Gospel tradition, while the preacher is concerned with its contemporary church setting, there is in principle no conflict between them. Indeed, the form-critical perspective can and should be a valuable one for preaching.

In the minds of most theological students and graduates of the past half century the names of Martin Dibelius and Rudolf Bultmann, especially the latter, are linked to the practice of form criticism and also to the historical skepticism about the Gospels which that discipline has been said to engender. Dibelius's form-critical book was translated into

English as early as the 1930s, perhaps because it was considered the less dangerous and radical of the two. Its title, *From Tradition to Gospel*, accurately conveys the intention and content of the book.[1] Bultmann's *The History of the Synoptic Tradition* was not translated until 1963,[2] more than forty years after the first German edition appeared. Perhaps by then the first rumblings of the death-of-God theology—not to mention such intervening events as World War II—had made Bultmann seem less nefarious by comparison.

The initial impact of form criticism on the American scene can be illustrated by one theological student's experience in the mid-1950s. I was introduced to Bultmann's criticism by polemics against it and did not really encounter Dibelius until I was a graduate student. Like many theological students I was warned about form criticism and to some extent protected from it. In the meantime I had been introduced to Albert Schweitzer by my teacher of theology, Robert E. Cushman, who made it very clear to us that Schweitzer had put an end to the liberal, historicist approach to the Gospels and to the theology that sought to build on that quicksand. From him and from W. D. Davies, my first New Testament teacher, we learned that the Gospels were scarcely biographical documents. Davies, a student of C. H. Dodd, was understandably prepared to stress the kerygmatic character of the Gospels, although he was certainly unwilling to engage in any wholesale depreciation of their historical witness. Through them and James T. Cleland, a trained New Testament scholar as well as a talented preacher, I first became aware of the possibilities this new approach offered for preaching. I must confess, however, that I was not prepared to pursue it at the time. Like so many of my contemporaries, professors and student colleagues, I myself was still almost entirely absorbed by the historical question of Jesus. In the aftermath of the challenges represented by Albert Schweitzer's apocalyptic interpretation of Jesus and Bultmann's apparent threat to dissolve him into the Gospel tradition, I was preoccupied with the following questions: What can we know? What is the theological status of our knowing or not knowing? These were, of course, important questions, and they still are. In theological school one ought to have the leisure to explore them—and not just over coffee but through encounter with serious books and biblical texts. I do not consider the time occupied with the question of the historical Jesus to have been misspent, but in ministry one cannot afford such leisure, or so it is thought. One now has to preach, and in some fashion to preach from the Gospels. So what happens?

From much preaching I have heard, by preachers both younger and older than myself, I can make a guess. My guess is that many preachers have left, and continue to leave, seminary in about the state I was in twenty-odd years ago. The important questions and issues represented by such names as Schweitzer and Bultmann have been raised, but answers—especially answers to so important a question as what all this has to do with preaching, *my* preaching—have not been forthcoming. Or if the answers have been perceived in principle, they have not taken root in practice. The result is that in preaching today the more difficult issues and texts are often not tackled. For example, we have learned that Mark 1:14–15 is central to an understanding of Mark and of the kingdom of God in Jesus' own thought. But how often is that or any other eschatologically oriented text actually preached? One may dare to preach on turning the cheek or on "Blessed are the poor in spirit, for theirs is the kingdom of heaven." But when one does, how often are these passages set in the context of Jesus' eschatology? I have heard them preached as sound advice or as general truths, but is it sound advice to turn the other cheek literally or figuratively against any kind of assault? I am not even sure that is good advice within the church's ministry. And it is no more obvious to me that the poor in spirit are receiving or finding the kingdom of heaven than it is that the meek are inheriting the earth or that those who are hungering and thirsting for righteousness, or for anything else, are being filled.

So often such texts as these are preached, but their eschatological premise is hidden. Thus the conceptual context in which they are meaningful remains obscure. Maybe—probably—it is known to the preacher, but it is allowed to remain hidden from the hearers. After nearly a century of preaching the friendly, accessible Jesus who conforms to our views and expectations, it is not surprising that many or most hearers, if left to their own devices, will understand these texts in exactly such an interpretative frame of reference. On this point there is no need to advocate a wholesale espousal of Schweitzer's views. Searching critical questions have been raised against his treatment of the Gospels and his formulation of Jesus' eschatology.[3] Nevertheless, such texts as these raise the fundamental eschatological question, that is, they are fundamental to understanding Jesus and early Christianity. What is then objectionable is a kind of preaching from such Gospel texts that does not let that issue, and other tough and potentially touchy but illuminating issues, come into view. I raise this matter not in the abstract but because of the preaching from the Gospels that I have heard for over forty years. Maybe such tough matters are avoided because we fear the reaction and outcome. People may leave the church, but under harmless, unchallenging, sometimes inane preaching people are leaving the church anyway. People continue to flock to fundamentalist, evangelical, or pentecostal churches and sects. Why? Is it because they are ignorant, hostile, in need of emotional release? Perhaps. But it may also have something to do with the fact that the emphasis on judgment and salvation in such churches strikes, if obliquely, the note of eschatological urgency that pervades the Gospels and the New Testament generally.

In his excellent book *The Bible in the Pulpit*, Leander Keck offers some perceptive comments on how and why the present situation has arisen. Among other things, he points out that the theological school itself, in teaching the methods and results of critical biblical study, has often succeeded in creating in students an ambivalence toward the Bible or an ambivalence toward biblical criticism or both.[4] As Keck observes, when students become pastors they may retreat from a critical perspective to a position in which they preach only from safe texts or treat their texts in a moralistic, ahistorical, or quasi-fundamentalist way. The latter is likely to happen to students whose native piety has disposed them to be skeptical of modern, historical methods of exegesis in the first place. Moreover, my own experience as a theological student may be far from unique. I seemed to be just at the point of being able to combine critical exegetical honesty with homiletical skill and pastoral insight when I graduated, without having done it enough to be affirmed and confident in it.

Without claiming to have a comprehensive cure for the maladies just described, I would like to suggest an approach to the Gospels that overcomes many of these problems and difficulties. We begin with the insight, engendered by form criticism and associated with the names of Dibelius and Dodd especially, that the Gospels are kerygmatic. That is, they are proclamation rather than biography. Of course, proclamation and biography are not necessarily mutually exclusive categories. Recent criticism has, in fact, moved back in the direction of asking "What is a gospel?" and answering that the gospel genre is not unrelated to ancient biography.[5] This shift in the tide of criticism is welcome. Nevertheless, the perception that the Gospels are not primarily biography, or that they are proclamation before they are biography, seems to me to be valid, necessary, and helpful, especially for preaching. When Dibelius writes that "missionary purpose was the cause and preaching was the means of spreading abroad that which the disciples of Jesus possessed as recollections,"[6] I may want to enter several addenda and questions. But the basic insight is sound. The function of the tradition (that is, recollections of Jesus) in the church, whether in missionary preaching, catechesis, or liturgy, fundamentally determined its content and shape. "Christian missionaries did not relate the life of Jesus, but proclaimed the salvation that had come about in Jesus," writes Dibelius. And he adds: "What they narrated was secondary to this proclamation, was intended to confirm and found it."[7] C. H. Dodd would have agreed heartily. Extending the sort of reasoning represented by the words of Dibelius, Dodd writes: "Mark therefore conceived himself as writing a form of *kerygma*, and that his Gospel is in fact a rendering of the apostolic preaching will become clear from an analysis of the book itself."[8]

These claims would be acknowledged by most working New Testament scholars today, even though they might want to expand their categories and qualify the emphasis on missionary preaching characteristic of Dibelius and Dodd. Yet the Gospels are in a real sense witness, and the material of the Gospels had its earliest use in the life of Christian churches. The primary task of the interpreter is to understand the Gospels as products of a churchly milieu. In their present form they are not witness to the unbelieving world, although the shape of that witness may well have influenced their form. They are, in all probability, addressed to the church, to believers. The Gospels cry out to be understood as products of the Christian faith within the Christian church.

A great many alarm bells were sounded when it was discovered that Rudolf Bultmann had written that the Gospels were primary sources for the historical situations which produced them, that is, for the early church, and only secondary sources for Jesus himself. (Actually, Bultmann credited Wellhausen with the insight "that a literary work or a fragment of tradition is a primary source for the historical situation out of which it arose, and is only a secondary source for the historical details concerning which it gives information.")[9] Bultmann's insight arose from his form-critical work. It was widely alleged that Bultmann regarded the Gospels as sources for the belief and piety of the early church but not for the historical Jesus. Anyone who has read Bultmann's own book on Jesus[10] knows very well that Bultmann believed that much could be said with a high degree of certainty about Jesus. The alarms were certainly overdone. Nevertheless, this bold statement could reasonably be put alongside Bultmann's other positions: the view, drawn from William Wrede, that Jesus probably did not claim to be the Messiah; the rejection of the historicity of the Gospel (Marcan) outline of Jesus' ministry, a position shared with Wrede and demonstrated by K. L. Schmidt; the belief that Jesus espoused a futuristic, apocalyptic eschatology, a view accepted from his own teacher Johannes Weiss as well as Schweitzer. This, taken together, may look like radical historical skepticism, which is exactly what Bultmann was and still is accused of. Yet all this does not necessarily belong together; the several positions do not require one another. Moreover, whether true or false, the debate over such matters should not be allowed to obscure the important and valid point that the Gospels are church books, that the church is, or was, their primary historical context. In content and shape, in form and function, they represent the interests and emphases of early Christian churches, and indeed of early Christian preaching. This is the basic discovery of form criticism.

What then is implied for our preaching from the Gospels? First, and perhaps most important, the form or genre of preaching is not foreign to the genre of gospel and the gospel tradition. The purpose of the stuff of which the Gospels are composed is also amenable to preaching, if it did not actually have its original *Sitz im Leben*, or setting in life, in the task of preaching, strictly speaking. When the pericopes of the Gospels are taken as texts for preaching, one is in close touch with their original intent and purpose.

John Knox once gave an interesting example of how this may be so.[11] Sketching the lines of exegesis of the pericope of Jesus' stilling the storm (Mark 4:35–41), he indicated that in its earliest form, probably even before its incorporation into the Gospel of Mark, this story was told to exemplify the Lord's saving work. It was already a text for preaching. Jesus saves, rescues, those (or the church) tossed about and endangered on the sea of life. Thus he raises with the disciples (and the church) the question of whether they have faith. Knox then recalled hearing his father preach on this same text in Georgia in the early part of this century. For his father too this story served as a text for preaching. He too saw its meaning in Jesus' rescuing the storm-tossed wanderers and questioning their faith. To the person who has eyes only for the historical question, who sees the text only as a witness to historical fact or a falsification of fact, such an interpretation looks like allegorical exegesis. But form criticism opens a way beyond literalist, biographical exegesis without encouraging flights of fanciful allegorizing.

Examples of form-critical analysis and interpretation of Gospel texts could be multiplied and extended, but they are plentifully available in the works already mentioned. Our point is not to do form criticism or to concern ourselves with form-critical categories as much as to underscore the importance of form criticism, particularly the value of its perspective. Through form criticism the nature of the Gospel material has been uncovered. One may in preaching decide to work with the form and meaning of a pericope in the pre-Gospel tradition, that is, at the form-critical level. That would be a legitimate procedure. More often than not, however, the preacher will and should inquire into the meaning of a story or saying in the Gospel of which it is a part. But that approach itself arises from insights into the Gospels that are based on form-critical and related studies. Such investigations led to the raising of fundamental questions about the nature of the Gospels and the justification or warrant for interpreting them as history, as biography, as theology, or whatever else.

We now turn to consider the character of the Gospel narratives. If one assumes, as modern Protestant interpreters have generally assumed, that the meaning of the biblical text is its literal meaning (that is, what the author meant to communicate), then it follows that the meaning of a narrative text in a Gospel is the literal meaning of the story. If the story purports to be true, historically factual, then the meaning of the text is bound up with the question of what actually happened. Did the wind and waves actually cease to roar? How may one then find warrant for an interpretation that does not first attend to, if not resolve, the question of what actually happened? The warrant for what might be called the historicist interpretation, that is, an interpretation which immediately places the Gospel text against the background of the historical circumstances of Jesus' ministry, is obvious, given a biographical-historical view of the Gospels.

But what if one does not adopt such a view? Immediately someone will ask, "Are the Gospels about Jesus or are they not? Do they recount what he actually said and did, or do they not?" Such a question, whether intentionally or not, reflects a historicist mentality. Not only is this so in that it insists on a positive answer to the historical question, but it is even more apparent in the unquestioned assumption that the historical question must be the *prior* question in the interpretation of a Gospel text. The really prior question of what sort of literature or material we are dealing with is ignored or hastily shoved aside. But there is no warrant for the priority of the historical question unless or until the nature of the text has been determined. Even if it is clear that we are here dealing with a narrative text, the relation that the text must have to history is not thereby given. Moreover, even if it is clear that the narrative text as a whole is about a historical person, and that his historicity and nature are germane to the text, even then the warrant for the priority of the historicist interpretation of a specific pericope is not established beyond all question. The warrants for the historicist interpretation of the story of the stilling of the storm are not necessarily given in the story itself. One has a right and an obligation to ask about the function of that story in the tradition, and therefore in the church, and in the Gospel in which it now stands. The raising and careful canvassing of these questions will prevent our jumping to conclusions which, however obvious they seem, may actually be hasty and ill-conceived. How a Gospel is to be understood, against what background, on the basis of what warrants—these are questions crucial for exegesis and for exegetically sound preaching. Here form criticism has played a seminal role.

We have so long thought of a Gospel as a continuous story of the life or at least the ministry of Jesus that we easily assume that what we are told is *all* that happened or *all* that was said. Form criticism has underscored what we might otherwise have realized, namely, that except in the passion narratives the successive pericopes of the Gospels do not necessarily represent successive events, the one following directly upon the other. For the most part, the pericopes are separate units with independent tradition histories. John makes clear (20:30–31; 21:25) that his Gospel is only a selection from among the many items which might have been recounted. From the very fact that all the Gospels present only a selection of Jesus' words and acts, it follows that by and large things are not given in their original, historical context. We have them in a literary, indeed, a theological, context. That is, we have them first of all in the canonical text. They have found their place there after a prior life in a social and cultic context, namely, in the early church's tradition.

It will be worthwhile to explain and expand upon this point. How are the literary contexts of the Gospels constructed? The synoptic framework—or itinerary, as it used to be called—of Jesus' ministry is fundamentally that of Mark. Both in wording and in order, Mark is frequently the middle term or common factor between Matthew and Luke. Most interpreters find it much easier to understand this state of affairs as resulting from Matthew's and Luke's use of Mark rather than from Mark's conflation of the other two Gospels. Yet Matthew and Luke, who relied upon and used Mark's account, obviously did not regard it as sacrosanct (Luke refers to his predecessors in 1:1). Each changed the order of events somewhat, Matthew more than Luke. For example, Matthew placed the Sermon on the Mount, which is largely his construction but which is based on an earlier tradition, at the beginning of Jesus' ministry, where it displaces the demon exorcism found in Mark, which has no exact Matthean parallel. For another example, Luke has Jesus' ministry begin with a long account of his rejection after preaching in the synagogue in Nazareth. This story, not found in its developed, Lucan form in Mark, is probably nevertheless based upon the much briefer narrative of Mark 6:1–6. (Later on, as he is closely following Mark's account, Luke omits that Marcan story; he has already used it.)

Mark's Gospel itself appears to be made up largely of groups or blocks of material of the same sort. After a typical day in the ministry of Jesus the Messiah (Mark 1:21–45), there comes a series of controversy stories (Mark 2:1—3:6). Mark 4 is a parable collection; in Mark 5 we find a series of mighty miracles. Mark 6 and 8 contain cycles of material centering about Jesus' feeding a large multitude of people. This is probably a doublet; that is, the two cycles are ultimately based on the same tradition or event. Mark 7 begins with a biting denunciation of the Pharisees and "the tradition of the elders" and ends with Jesus' single foray into Gentile territory. Mark 8–10 centers about or continually reverts to the theme of Jesus' suffering messiahship and the sort of discipleship for which it calls. Mark 12 is mostly a series of controversy stories once again, and Mark 13 is an apocalyptic discourse. Obviously much if not most of the material in Mark is grouped topically or according to type or form. It is not in chronological order and, at least in large part, does not directly reflect the historical context of Jesus' own ministry. Papias in the second century describes Mark as having written down the preaching of Peter, but not in order; in principle that is not a bad description.

We have been dealing only with the synoptics. John, of course, presents a vastly different itinerary and order of events and creates enormous difficulties for anyone bent on reading the Gospels as chronologically accurate, historical documents. Much ingenuity has been devoted to resolving the discrepancies between John and the synoptics. Actually they are in all likelihood beyond resolution. (See below, chapter 9.)

The point is not that some or most of the things recounted in the Gospels did not happen. Some probably did not happen, but many did. The point is that we do not have them narrated in their original order and historical context. We have them instead as the result of the stories and sayings having been transmitted, probably at first orally, in the preaching, teaching, and other functions of the churches. We have them as they have been next incorporated into written documents, the Gospels. They have, or have had, traditional contexts and literary contexts. Since it is in those contexts that we have the sayings and stories about Jesus, we do not have direct access to their historical context, the *Sitz im Leben Jesu* (setting in the life of Jesus). What we are given in the Gospels is the literary setting of a saying or story, and in this literary setting we are closer to the setting in the history of the early church than to the earlier setting in Jesus' ministry.

This point can be illustrated and supported by two examples, one from contemporary scholarship and the other from the text of Mark. The learned and somewhat conservative scholar Joachim Jeremias has written a standard work in the field in *The Parables of Jesus*.[12] Jeremias's purpose in that work is to use the linguistic erudition and form-critical procedures at his disposal to elucidate the original form of the parables of Jesus. He is confident that this can be done with a reasonable degree of certainty. He is equally certain, however, that we do not presently have the parables in their original contexts and that therefore to a certain extent we do not have them in their original form. We have them in the Gospels in the form in which they were transmitted by the evangelists. That we do not in all probability have them in their original context can be shown from Matthew's and Luke's different uses of parables common to them only. For example, Matthew puts the parable of the talents into his apocalyptic discourse (that is, in Jerusalem), but Luke has Jesus tell it between Jericho and Jerusalem (before he reaches Jerusalem). Matthew puts the parable of the marriage feast after the triumphal entry, when Jesus is in Jerusalem (Matt. 22:1–10); Luke has his similar parable in the journey section, when Jesus is presumably well away from Jerusalem (Luke 14:15–24).

Jeremias thus sets about to recover the original settings and meanings of the parables. Linguistic and formal considerations are a great help, but of paramount importance is the insight that Jesus proclaimed the inbreaking of the kingdom of God. The parables were originally spoken in that eschatological context, but the church has tended to domesticate them for purposes of ethical instruction. That process is seen to be at work already in the Gospels. Eschatological urgency is a mark of genuineness, and the mission to proclaim the kingdom's dawning frequently provides the probable original context in Jesus' ministry and teaching. But the exact chronological historical context of the parables is still for the most part lost to us. If, however, we can be reasonably sure of a parable's original meaning, its interpretation in the church's tradition, and its literary context in the Gospels, that is ample basis and material for exegesis and preaching.

To turn to the example from Mark, it is obviously true that no single text or pericope can be interpreted independently of its literary context. Mark, or someone, has presumably put the Gospel together in the way he has for a purpose. But, as we have just seen, one cannot assume that the Marcan literary context is also the historical context. Mark 3:2 tells of people, apparently Pharisees (v. 6), watching to see whether Jesus would heal a man with a withered hand on the Sabbath so that they might accuse him. Just previously in Mark's account, in response to the controversy in the grainfields Jesus has replied to some Pharisees, "The sabbath was made for man, not man for the sabbath; so the Son of man is lord even of the sabbath" (Mark 2:27–28). The two passages are unquestionably related thematically and in the composition of Mark's Gospel. It is far less certain, however, that they originally occurred in this order, assuming both represent a genuine authentic situation and word of Jesus. Probably they were originally transmitted independently. In other words, it is scarcely safe to suppose that Jesus approached the man with the withered hand with the incident in the grainfields on his mind, or that the Pharisees who are appalled at Jesus' healing the man are the same Pharisees who shortly before had accosted him, or his disciples, in the fields. Thus speculation about what Jesus may have been thinking about the previous incident as he dealt with the situation of the man with the withered hand is fruitless and really beside the point. It is hard enough to know what Jesus was thinking within one situation described in a Gospel; the evangelists do not provide access to his psyche. The difficulty is compounded when one attempts to relate Jesus', or his interlocutors', attitude in one pericope to what takes place in the next. We know the literary context, Mark; we can make a surmise about the traditional context, the preaching and teaching of early Christian churches. It is much more hazardous to make inferences about the meaning of the text on the basis of any presumed situation in the life of Jesus. More often than not we simply do not know. Yet just this is still done frequently in preaching.

It is instructive to note that Zeffirelli's recent television film *Jesus of Nazareth* deals with the order of events or pericopes of the canonical Gospels with much the same freedom as the evangelists deal with their tradition, or as Matthew and Luke treat Mark.[13] With great freedom and even license, he moves pericopes about so that all that is left from any of the Gospels is the most general order of events: baptism by John, the calling of the disciples, teaching and miracles, plotting against Jesus, passion and resurrection. Not even the confession of Peter really retains the central and pivotal position it had in Mark. (Zeffirelli also sometimes breaks up and changes pericopes and traditional complexes in a manner not unlike the apocryphal gospels; for example, the Sermon on the Mount is broken up, and Jesus' word about the law from Matt. 5:17 is put into the mouth of John the Baptist.) Zeffirelli's motivations were presumably to get certain materials in, while leaving others out; to narrate a historically plausible story; and to create an artistic work satisfying to the viewer. Whatever his motivations, and however different they may have been from those of the evangelists, Zeffirelli seems to have shared in significant ways these perspectives and goals. He did not regard the traditional context of the various sayings, stories, or parables as inviolable; that is, he did not regard the order of any one of the Gospels as binding. He felt free to arrange the material in a new way in order to present the picture of Jesus which he intended and which he doubtless felt was in some significant sense a true one. In these respects he did not differ in principle from the canonical evangelists.

Therefore, one cannot emphasize too strongly that the context of a

Gospel passage about which we may have the most certainty in exegesis and preaching is *not* the context of Jesus' historical ministry but that of the individual Gospel or Gospels in which it appears. About the original historical context we have the least certainty, and one can usually do no more than generalize. Thus, for example, one can agree with Jeremias that eschatology, the proclamation of the dawn of the kingdom, provides the general context for the interpretation of many of Jesus' parables. But by and large we do not know the chronological or more exact situational context within his ministry. Thus, surmises about that context—much less speculations about it—that are not firmly rooted in a critical understanding of the text are likely to do more harm than good. They are more likely to lead us *away* from the real Jesus—who is also the risen Jesus of the church's faith and proclamation—than *to* him. When I hear such statements as "Now Jesus certainly had this in mind...," or "What Jesus surely wanted to do was this...," or "Jesus, knowing what his disciples would need to prepare them for ministry, said...," I am forewarned that what I am likely to hear is not Jesus but the opinion and perhaps the unbridled imagination of the preacher. It is so easy to slip ourselves into the text, so that the danger that Paul feared, of preaching ourselves rather than Christ as Lord (2 Cor. 4:5), becomes real. There is so much to preach on in the Bible, the New Testament, and the Gospels. We do not need to make things up.

One obvious question in preaching from the Gospels is how the text or pericope may be delimited. We have not addressed this question directly, but the discussion of form criticism affords a useful vantage point from which to consider it. Anyone with theological or similar training will appreciate the importance of viewing in its proper literary and theological context the portion of the Gospel that is to be used in preaching. Form criticism helps both in delimiting the pericope and in establishing that context.

In the synoptic Gospels the discrete units of tradition that may be established by form-critical considerations are usually identical with the narrative or sense units—that is, a miracle story, a parable, a pronouncement story so-called. The paragraphing of a modern version of the Bible, such as the Revised Standard Version, is a reasonably good guide to these traditional sense units. But one must always be aware that a traditional unit may span more than one paragraph of a version, or that a single paragraph may contain more than one traditional unit.

The lectionary, especially contemporary lectionaries formed or revised under the influence of modern biblical scholarship, will prove useful in establishing the pericope, but even these cannot be used uncritically. In the delimitation of a pericope for preaching, one should exercise an informed, critical judgment in following a lectionary. It cannot even be assumed that there is in every case only one correct delimitation of each pericope. Nevertheless, preaching from the Gospels, as from any biblical text, requires that the question of the extent of the text be the subject of serious analysis and reflection.

Lectionaries ordinarily specify an Epistle and an Old Testament text as well as a Gospel text for a given Sunday or other occasion. This fact raises another interesting and important question: Should the preacher attempt to preach from, or incorporate, elements from all three readings in a sermon? There is a sense in which such combinations of Gospel, Epistle, and Old Testament lections afford a new hermeneutical context, not explicitly given in Scripture, for the interpretation of the individual texts. Such combinations then represent a kind of canon within the canon. This is not necessarily bad, although the reader or hearer should be aware of what is going on. A sensible rule of thumb would seem to be that the sermon, if it is expository, should be based primarily on one passage only, although all lectionary passages read in the service might well be referred to or alluded to in the course of preaching. The reasons for this rule as far as the Gospels are concerned are spelled out in the final section of this book. For the moment, two observations will suffice: First, a single Gospel (or other) pericope ordinarily provides more than ample food for exegesis and preaching. Second, the attempt to deal with two texts in one sermon can easily lead to the distortion of one or both, or their combination on the basis of some extrinsic principle foreign to the essential burden or thrust of either. It should be reiterated, however, that this is a rule of thumb rather than an ironclad principle.[14]

Most newer lectionaries encompass a three-year cycle, in which parallel synoptic renditions of the same event or saying sometimes occur (for example, the confession of Peter in Matthew and Mark). They thus imply that the preacher is to take cognizance of the various ways in which the several evangelists employ the same traditions. This aspect of Gospel study is the province of the discipline known as redaction criticism, to which we now turn.

3

THE GOSPELS AS
THE EVANGELISTS' PREACHING:
REDACTION CRITICISM

THE IMPORTANCE of form criticism for understanding the character and content of the Gospels is real. Form criticism underscores the
point that the substance of the Gospels has been shaped by the interests
and functions of the early church. For example, who can doubt that the
setting of the words of institution of the Lord's Supper was preserved in
the liturgy of the church before being incorporated into the Gospels?
The variations we find in the New Testament and in later books of
worship can often be traced to liturgical use. Bultmann's view that the
Gospel material testifies first to the setting in which it was preserved and
transmitted and only secondarily to the events or scenes it narrates is
true in at least this sense: so far as the individual pericopes and sayings
are concerned, the context or setting closer to us is that of the church or
churches that preserved and transmitted the still earlier Jesus traditions.

It is form criticism (or form history) which has led us to this conclusion. While I find its general perspective and insights helpful, in the very
nature of the case a great deal is left to hypothesis or conjecture. For
good reason the practitioners of the art disagree among themselves.
One's view of the forms and character of the material preserved and the
modes of transmission will be governed in large measure by one's view
of Christian origins and the nature of the early church. Bultmann,
Dibelius, and W. D. Davies see the early church generally as deeply
pervaded by eschatology, pneumatology, and mission. Accordingly, in
their view the shape and stability of the tradition is heavily influenced by
such factors. On the other hand, Birger Gerhardsson insists on a rabbinic model of the early church's teaching office administered by an

apostolic college in Jerusalem.[1] Along with that goes a conservative handling and evaluation of the tradition. In his recent fascinating study, Gerd Theissen has advanced the thesis that the earliest tradition had its setting in the activity of itinerant, charismatic preachers like Jesus himself.[2] Thus the shape and content of the tradition—for example, its frequent references to homelessness and cutting family ties—is directly related to the fact that it was preserved and purveyed by such wandering Palestinian preachers. Theissen correctly observes that this thesis in itself says nothing about the authenticity of the tradition. Yet he apparently finds it congenial with the view that in large measure the material of the tradition emanates from Jesus himself. In such a fluid setting, however, one would scarcely expect the tradition to be strictly and zealously monitored, as would be the case on Gerhardsson's view.

But such differences of scholarly opinion pose a problem. Most preachers probably feel that they themselves are not expert and cannot become expert in the intricacies and fine nuances of New Testament scholarship in general and form criticism in particular. Therefore, they do not feel qualified to adjudicate among the experts. Moreover, these are all matters that congregations know next to nothing about. How can one expect to inform them, perhaps against their will? This is more than the preacher can reasonably be expected to cope with. Yet the dilemma may not be as hopeless as it at first appears.

To begin with, one need not assume responsibility for more than one text or pericope at a time. The important thing is not to have comprehensive solutions in hand but to be knowledgeable about the likeliest possibilities for understanding and interpreting a specific text. Of course, while the preacher is not responsible for all the Gospels or all possible texts at once, this does not mean that a text can be treated in isolation. To be responsible for one text means to be able to analyze it and to think in an informed way about it. One does not have to be able to fit it into a predetermined or fixed view of the Gospels, the New Testament, or Christian origins in order to be able to preach from it. It is, however, important to know the issues surrounding a text in order to preach from it responsibly: What use did a story or saying have in the early churches? What is its probable relationship to Jesus himself? Fully to air and entertain such questions should be illuminating and helpful for preaching. It is not necessary to be able to answer every question posed by a text to be able to preach from it. Moreover—and this is particularly important—preaching from a text is not the same as offering critically informed opinions about it. Preaching should be based upon exegesis, and sermons may contain exegesis, but preaching is not the same as historical-critical exegesis. Exegesis should inform the preacher and thus inform preaching. As superfluous or ridiculous as it may sound to say it, one does not preach form criticism or any other criticism. To anyone who says, "I can't preach form criticism to my congregation," one must reply, "Of course you can't preach it to them, but that does not mean you can or should preach without it."

We began by discussing historical problems, or problems in preaching from the Gospels as straight historical accounts. We then saw the necessity of taking account of the traditional character of the material of which the Gospels are composed. All this is nothing new. Anyone who has graduated from an American theological seminary within the last fifty years should have some appreciation of the historical problems. Almost anyone who has graduated from an American theological seminary within the past quarter of a century, indeed, since World War II, will have felt the impact of form criticism for weal or woe. The latter period, which saw the wide dissemination of form-critical results and perspectives, also witnessed the appearance, again in Germany, of what has come to be known as redaction criticism. If Bultmann and Dibelius were the fathers of the form-critical or tradition-historical perspective and method in Gospel study, they were the grandfathers of redaction criticism. Their students, especially Bultmann's, pioneered the development of redaction criticism as a self-conscious method of Gospel study.

While it took the historical and form-critical initiatives of continental scholarship a quarter- to a half-century to be felt in the English-speaking world, redaction criticism spread much faster. There were at least two reasons for this. In the first place, all sorts of cultural transactions between Europe and America took place at a much faster pace after World War II. I can remember my first visit to Europe in the early 1960s and my own amazement at how Americanized the European commerce and popular culture seemed in contrast to my expectations. "Alles schrecklich in Deutschland kommt aus Amerika" (Everything terrible in Germany comes from America), a famous German theologian once said. Some might want to return the compliment as far as biblical scholarship is concerned. Yet the influence of the German scene upon us is undeniable and on the whole necessary and even beneficial. In any event, redaction-critical works were read and quickly translated in America and Great Britain. As a matter of fact, it was soon discovered that something like redaction criticism had already been going on in the English-speaking world. We just didn't have a German word for it.

In the second place, while the results of form criticism were at first viewed with foreboding, redaction criticism seemed full of potential for theology and preaching. The reasons for the initially negative and positive reactions are not difficult to determine. Form criticism seemed to cut away at the historical foundations of the Gospels and to make the subject matter of the Gospels, Jesus, less accessible for Christian faith. A good part of the negative historical attitudes of some form critics were given in the historical presuppositions of their work and were not entirely the result of the application of form-critical method. Nevertheless, form criticism understandably focused attention on negative judgments about the authenticity of stories and sayings of Jesus, although this was not its fundamental intention or significance.

Redaction criticism did not carry with it the same negative theological or historical baggage. The basic insight of redaction criticism was that the evangelists were authors and theologians painting their own portraits of Jesus and addressing themselves to important theological issues, albeit in the church of the first century. It had an obvious, immediate, and positive theological bearing on the task of exegesis and preaching; indeed, it made solid contact with established exegetical principles. Calling upon no less orthodox a father of the church than Athanasius, Pope Pius XII's encyclical *Divino Afflante Spiritu,* promulgated in 1943, had already expressed quite aptly the need and justification of redaction criticism:

> Let the interpreter then, with care and without neglecting any light derived from recent research, endeavor to determine the peculiar character and circumstances of the sacred writer, the age in which he lived, and the sources written or oral to which he had recourse and the forms of expression he employed.
>
> Thus can he the better understand who was the inspired author, and what he wishes to express by his writings. There is no one indeed but knows that the supreme rule of interpretation is to discover and define what the writer intended to express, as St. Athanasius excellently observes: "Here, as indeed is expedient in all other passages of Sacred Scripture, it should be noted, on what occasion the Apostle spoke; we should carefully and

faithfully observe to whom and why he wrote, lest, being ignorant of these points, or confounding one with the other, we miss the real meaning of the author."[3]

Redaction critics might have relatively high, or relatively low, estimates of the historical trustworthiness of the material conveyed in the Gospels. They were, however, willing to bracket out the historical question, in a way which critics could scarcely do, in order to pursue the intention and meaning of the evangelists. "The question of what really happened," writes Willi Marxsen, "is excluded from the outset. We inquire rather how the evangelists describe what happened."[4] Or, as Conzelmann put it in his work on Luke, "We must make it plain ... that our aim is to elucidate Luke's work in its present form, not to inquire into possible sources or into the historical facts which provide the material."[5] (In fact, both Marxsen and Conzelmann had a relatively low view of the historicity of the Gospels, but their work could be appropriated by scholars and interpreters who did not agree with them on this point.)

Redaction critics stressed the insight that all the Gospels, especially the synoptics, are based upon or arise out of three settings in life. First, there is the setting of Jesus' actual historical ministry. This setting was real, and its importance is not to be dismissed. The reality of that historical setting is indispensable to Christian faith as we know it. In the case of most stories and sayings of Jesus, however, that *Sitz im Leben* is impossible to reconstruct except in a general way. Second, there is the setting in the life of the early church which preserved the Gospel tradition. Without doubt, tradition was preserved and transmitted because it performed a valued function in the religious community. Third, we have the situation of the evangelist himself. That situation in each case gave rise to the Gospels. The Gospels are not to be viewed as the products of that situation pure and simple; they are more than the last stage in the development of the tradition in the church. (That was Bultmann's position, which Marxsen, among others, attacks.) Rather, the Gospels are the works of individual authors and are therefore something more and other than the sum totals of their traditional parts at a relatively late stage of development.

From the perspective of redaction criticism, interpretation has two foci. On the one hand, there is the situation of an early Christian church, in which the evangelist lived and worked; it may be presumed that he addressed himself to the problems, needs, and issues of that church. On the other hand, one must reckon with the individuality and even the literary skill of the author; while he speaks from and to that situation as he perceives it, his composition is far more than a reflex of that situation, as a close analysis of the text will show. He works with tradition. The insights of form criticism about the discrete, individual blocks of the tradition as preserved and transmitted are not abandoned. Yet one perceives that the author works with that tradition in fresh and creative ways. He does something new and different. This is particularly true of Mark. The evangelist is genuinely an author. While his literary creativity is limited by tradition and church, it is nevertheless a factor to be reckoned with.

Intriguing though it may be, the situational pole of redaction criticism is its more problematic aspect, while the analysis of the text itself is fortunately more basic to the task. The text, after all, lies before us; certain things about it will be obvious. It is a narrative; it is organized in a certain way; the individual episodes, except perhaps for the passion, are relatively independent units. If the generally accepted results of New Testament scholarship are adopted, the narratives of Matthew and Luke will be viewed as based on that of Mark. If a form-critical perspective is embraced, the individual pericopes will be viewed as having taken shape and been transmitted in the tradition of the early church. (Thus the structure and to some extent the nature of the author's sources can rather quickly be agreed upon.) Moreover, if it is correct that the tradition circulated in the form of individual stories and sayings, it is likely that the redactional or editorial work of the evangelist can be most readily observed at the interstices, the seams, of the pericopes. Redaction criticism narrowly conceived concentrates primarily upon the task of distinguishing tradition from redaction in order to understand the author's purpose as it is reflected in his editing. We shall in the next chapter observe how the distinction of redaction from tradition may be helpful in interpretation.

Redaction criticism more broadly conceived (sometimes called "composition criticism") does not, however, rely solely or even primarily on this distinction, which from case to case is only more or less probable. Rather, the critic looks also at the document—in this case the Gospel—as a totality. A particular pericope or text may be singled out for attention, but it is not examined solely with a view to analyzing its components. It must be studied so that its relation to the work of which it is a part is understood. One must ask how or to what extent it represents or conveys the typical emphases of the work as a whole, and how it fits into its composition or structure. So, on the one hand, the interpreter asks about the character of a Gospel and the function of a particular pericope within it. Thus he deals not only with the question of tradition and redaction but also with matters of thematic emphasis (What theological or other ideas are central?) and compositional structure and style (How does understanding the composition of this Gospel contribute to its interpretation?). On the other hand, the interpreter does not lose sight of the challenging if problematic task of imaginatively conceiving and reconstructing the historical setting in which and for which the evangelist wrote.

In order to give concreteness and specificity to these principles or methods, let us look at a large section of the Gospel of Mark.

Structural considerations show that Mark 8:22—10:52 is the central part of the Gospel. This long midsection begins with the story of the blind man who at first sees men like trees walking. It ends with the gift of sight to blind Bartimaeus, who then chooses to follow Jesus. Before this point in the Gospel is reached, Jesus' miracles are recounted in great numbers and much detail. His teaching is frequently mentioned but not extensively given or described, except in controversial scenes like Mark 7:1–23, when Jesus denounces the Pharisees and the tradition of the elders. Mark contains a number of controversy scenes and stories. These bear some relationship to the demon exorcisms, which are characterized by struggle between the demons and Jesus. But Mark 8:22–26 introduces a section in which decisive new factors enter the picture. First, in response to Jesus' question Peter confesses Jesus as Messiah (Mark 8:27–30). Then Jesus repeatedly predicts his approaching suffering and death as the Son of man (Mark 8:31; 9:31; 10:33–34). Jesus appears transfigured before his disciples (Mark 9:2–8), but the disciples are far from understanding the meaning of this and other things that are transpiring, or what Jesus is saying. Indeed, the whole section mirrors and emphasizes the disciples' lack of understanding, both of Jesus and of themselves. This is nowhere more clearly the case than in those instances in which Jesus instructs them in the meaning of discipleship (Mark 8:31–38; 9:33–37; 10:35–45). When the disciples, or James and John, seek preferment, Jesus admonishes them by his own example: "Whoever would be great among you must be your servant, and whoever would be first among you must be slave of all. For the Son of man came also not to be served but to serve, and to give his life as a ransom for many" (Mark 10:43–45).

Immediately after this central, pivotal section of Mark, Jesus enters Jerusalem (Mark 11:1–11) and the passion week is already beginning. We are clearly now in a new stage of the narration and a new major section of the Gospel. The structure, the arrangement of the material, and the emphases that emerge in the narrative show that a distinctive teaching about messiahship and discipleship is being set forth and emphasized in Mark 8:22—10:52. The theme of the true character of Jesus' messiahship leads over to the reiterated and heavily emphasized teaching about discipleship.

Remembering what we know about early Christianity, and observing the way Mark first presents Jesus as a mighty miracle worker and controversialist, inspired and empowered by God, what do we make of this sudden shift of emphasis? An earlier generation might have said that Jesus, aware of the impression made by his miracles, did not want himself or his messiahship to be misunderstood by his disciples. But however that may be, according to Mark's portrayal they continued to misunderstand, despite Jesus' very explicit statements to them. Furthermore, Mark doesn't give us a clue about Jesus' personal intention or motivation. To speak of what Jesus himself thought raises a whole series of problems that we need not go into here. But if we stay with Mark and his purpose and intention, we can make important progress in the text and Mark's own situation. By arranging and formulating the material at his disposal, Mark has suggested that discipleship, distinctively Christian discipleship, means following Jesus in the path to the cross (Mark 8:34) rather than the performance of mighty works. Why does Mark do this? To whom does he intend to speak?

As we noted, the most challenging and problematic aspect of redaction criticism comes at the point of imagining and reconstructing the *Sitz im Leben* of the evangelist, the church situation out of which and to which he speaks. It may be important for the redaction critic to be able to establish the situation, for any specific purpose of the evangelist will be integrally linked to it. Thus the reading and interpretation of texts will be influenced in an important way by the interpreter's understanding of the situation and problems being addressed by the evangelist. At just this point there arises the greatest difference of opinion among redaction critics. That this should be the case is entirely understandable. If there is one thing that is not patent or obvious in the Gospels it is the historical situations to which they are addressed. It does not follow that they are *not* addressed to a specific setting and purpose. Nevertheless, the fact that they are Gospels, that is, narratives of Jesus' ministry, means that their own contemporary situations can be expressed or reflected only indirectly in the text; they must be inferred from the content, construction, redaction, and apparent emphases of the narrative. To do that is not an easy task. Yet it is not impossible, particularly if one does not insist on being able to reconstruct the specifics of the evangelist's situation too precisely.

The reconstruction of the historical situation of the author can, moreover, be important for preaching. Let me attempt to specify and illustrate how this may be so. In light of Mark 8:22—10:52, it may be argued that the Gospel of Mark is addressed to a church in which there was great preoccupation with the miraculous or charismatic as the attestation of Jesus' messiahship and the hallmark of discipleship. Certainly Mark's tradition was heavily freighted with such things as miracles and demon exorcisms. Down to Mark 8:22 the Gospel is dominated by this material. Apparently Mark himself credited these phenomena fully as historical occurrences. Clearly Acts and Paul's letters indicate that such occurrences were common enough, or at least believed to be common, in the primitive church. Early Christianity was not a movement of philosophers and their students. It was charismatic, inspired, eschatologically oriented. From the outside it may well have appeared to have more in common with certain cults of our day than with the so-called main-line churches. Not without some reason did the authorities regard early Christianity as a dangerous or potentially dangerous movement. From a different perspective, it becomes understandable why biblically inspired revivals within the main-line churches are sometimes accompanied by charismatic attitudes and activity and a revived interest in eschatology. Such things were characteristic of early Christian life. Mark seems to reflect and recognize this. Moreover, he acknowledges and amply demonstrates that these things were rooted in the ministry of Jesus himself. Mark does not deny the miraculous, the charismatic, or the eschatological, yet he accepts them only in their proper place. They are to be seen in the perspective of the cross and the understanding of messiahship and discipleship implicit in it. Mark draws out this understanding in 8:22—10:52.

If Mark was in fact addressing himself to a church in which the tradition of Jesus as wonder-worker and charismatic leader was dominant, his emphasis on the meaning of the cross in relation to discipleship—that it implies suffering and service for the disciple as well as for the Christ—is further illumined. We know that the danger or potential danger of viewing Christian life as the triumph over and freedom from the conditions and limitations of historical existence already existed in the early church. That being the case, the Marcan emphasis would answer to it. Moreover, this emphasis quite possibly reflects a specific historical circumstance which Mark the evangelist knew and to which he intended to speak.

We seem to have come upon a situation in which Mark stands over against his tradition, that is, the tradition of miracles and related phenomena. More accurately, he interprets some parts of his tradition in the light of other parts. He interprets the miracle-working Jesus in light of the Son of man who suffers and dies for his followers. Thus Jesus himself becomes the paradigm of discipleship for a church that is in danger of misunderstanding him, or the gospel, because of a one-sided emphasis on that sort of empowerment which is not distinctively Christian, not subject to the proper theological understanding of suffering and the cross. Against such a historical background the purpose and theology of Mark stand out in bold relief. For Mark, Jesus' suffering and death are central to his messianic role. Although the disciples could not understand this during Jesus' ministry, they presumably came to such an understanding in the light of the subsequent crucifixion and resurrection. In any event, Mark presents such an understanding as central and fundamental to Christian discipleship.

Having briefly set forth this assessment of the historical situation and purpose of Mark as reflected in this central section, let us return to the contemporary task of preaching. How is this determination relevant to that task? What bearing does it have on the task of preaching?

Starting with the last question—What bearing does it have on the task of preaching?—let us quickly concede that the authority of the text does not, in principle, depend on our ability to determine its function and intention in a historical setting. But the meaning of the text may depend on it, or at least be supported by it. Without a conception of that situation the text may prove mute or even misleading. What is the meaning of this central complex of Mark's Gospel? If by this is meant, What was the intention of the author with respect to the readers he could envision? then knowledge of the situation of those readers, as well as of the direction in which he intended to lead them, is germane to an understanding of the text. If the assessment of that situation we have suggested is correct, then Mark intends to lead his readers away from a misappropriation of the tradition of Jesus' miracles as central to the meaning of the gospel and toward an appreciation of the meaning of the cross, not only for Christology but for their own lives as well. Since this section of Mark's Gospel is not only central structurally but also central to his understanding of the gospel message, the interpretation of the whole of Mark's Gospel should conform to its meaning or bearing. That is, if we are to be true to Mark's intention, we can never ignore it, not even when dealing with a miracle story. In fact, we can afford to ignore it least of all when dealing with a miracle story.

Thus it is possible already to see the relevance of the historical situation of Mark, and the purpose with which he addressed it, to the task of preaching. Not only will the meaning of Mark historically be understood more clearly if this situation can be established, but the preacher may also gain from this knowledge some guidance and help in preaching to the congregation. We preachers need to ask ourselves what are the analogies between Mark and our own preaching on the one hand and between Mark's situation and the congregation to which we speak on the other. Is there in the congregation an emphasis on miracles, charismatic power, and demon exorcism that is getting out of hand? Does one at least need to measure and evaluate such manifestations against the sign of the cross? Twenty or more years ago the answer would have been no, and the preacher would have begun looking for some other valid analogy. Today, however, many congregations are preoccupied by just such manifestations of spiritual power, which need constantly to be assessed against the center of the gospel's message. Scripture is like a good piece of old clothing. Just keep it and it will come back in style. But the actual analogies to Mark's situation may not lie in the same realm of spiritual empowerment. A more prevalent and relevant analogy may be found in the organization and life of our established churches. Not threatened by civil authority or social disapproval, perhaps smug in the confidence that the demons of personal vice and social unjustice have been thoroughly exorcised from our midst, we may nevertheless be in need of the jolting juxtaposition of that attitude (or tradition) with the message of the cross. In either case the preacher would want to go with the *direction* of the text. Insofar as redaction criticism is concerned, this means uncovering the purpose of the evangelist, his intention in addressing his readers. What is his tendency? What is the drift, or better the thrust, of his thought? One might well preach a sermon on one of the Marcan miracle or exorcism stories, using it as a basis for speaking of the power of Christ or the empowerment of the believer. Such talk would go astray only if it were not qualified by the message of suffering service, which was Mark's understanding of the meaning of the cross, and of the gospel itself.

At this point we ask again whether or in what sense a determination of the historical situation of the evangelist is indispensable to preaching. Could not one have said what has been said about Mark without reference to that situation? The answer is both yes and no. Yes, one could have said it. On the view that Jesus is the "redactor" of Mark, that is, that Mark expresses Jesus' intention over against his original disciples, much the same viewpoint has been set forth. Jesus warns his disciples that the gospel is centered in suffering and death, not in miracles. In fact, one test of any proposed historical situation is to ask whether it helps explain the text as it stands. The view that Jesus is the "redactor" does help explain the text's fundamental theological intention. Mark intends us to believe that he is conveying the truth of Jesus and the gospel, not his own truth. Therefore, if it works to view Jesus as redactor, this means that Mark has composed his work exactly as intended, so that the purpose of Jesus might shine through. And I believe he did. Yet as we have observed, the view that it all goes back directly to Jesus presents historical problems. The text is difficult to explain as straight, historical narrative of Jesus' time. Among other things, Jesus says things plainly which the disciples appear not to hear. Such difficulties necessarily get in the way of any interpreter who is responsible to modern biblical study. But a genuine, that is, theologically valid, reading of the text is not impossible apart from redaction-critical insight into the nature of the church situation of the author and his intention in addressing it.

On the other hand, valid preaching could not take place apart from some determination about who or what is being addressed in the text. If redaction criticism reconstructs the historically original purpose of the text, it is playing an indispensable role in the interpretation of the text. If without such redactional analysis and reconstruction valid interpretations of the text have been given, in preaching or elsewhere, that is only because the audience and aim of the text has otherwise been correctly imagined and construed. That can happen because Mark portrays Jesus and the original disciples as standing in exactly the same relation as Mark's Gospel and the first-century church for which he writes. As Jesus admonished his disciples, so Mark admonishes the church. Thus, if readers rightly understand the narrative and relate themselves to it, they grasp the thrust of what is said about the centrality of suffering and the cross by putting themselves in the place of the disciples being addressed by Jesus. But aside from any historical problems, on that narrative level the situation of Jesus and his disciples can all too easily be viewed as an isolated event rather than as archetypical of the relationship between the gospel and the believer, who is constantly subject to temptation. That is, it can become a once-for-all event in the sense of an artifact of the past.

Redaction criticism, as the attempt to reconstruct the audience of a text so that the historically intended meaning of the text (that is, of the evangelist) may stand out in relief, is then at least a useful, practical hermeneutical discipline or tool. By using it we can better see where and at what the text is aimed, and we can then stand in the way of it and bring our congregations into its line of fire. Otherwise, we may—to stretch a metaphor—point the text up into the air and scatter our shot.

PART TWO

Preaching from
the Synoptic Gospels:
Some Paradigms and Specimens

4

PREACHING FROM MARK

W E HAVE now looked at preaching from the Gospels from a number of perspectives: the historical, the tradition-critical (form-critical), and the redaction-critical. In doing so, the problems and limitations—but also the opportunities and challenges—of preaching from the Gospels became apparent.

At this point it will be profitable to take a text of preachable length from one of the Gospels and to look at it from all the perspectives we have just considered. Then we shall ask ourselves how it will preach or how one should preach it. We take from the larger, central section of Mark, just considered, a text that is obviously Marcan in its theme and emphases. Perhaps nothing could be more typical of Mark than Peter's confession:

> And Jesus went on with his disciples, to the villages of Caesarea Philippi; and on the way he asked his disciples, "Who do men say that I am?" And they told him, "John the Baptist; and others say, Elijah; and others one of the prophets." And he asked them, "But who do you say that I am?" Peter answered him, "You are Christ." And he charged them to tell no one about him.
>
> And he began to teach them that the Son of man must suffer many things, and be rejected by the elders and the chief priests and the scribes, and be killed, and after three days rise again. And he said this plainly. And Peter took him, and began to rebuke him. But turning and seeing his disciples, he rebuked Peter, and said, "Get behind me, Satan! For you are not on the side of God, but of men."
>
> And he called to him the multitude with his disciples, and said to them, "If any man would come after me, let him deny himself and take up his cross and follow me. For whoever would save his life will lose it; and whoever loses his life for my sake and the gospel's will save it. For what does it profit a man, to gain the whole world and forfeit his life? For what can a man give in return for his life? For whoever is ashamed of me and of my words in this adulterous and sinful generation, of him will the Son of

man also be ashamed, when he comes in the glory of his Father with the holy angels."

And he said to them, "Truly, I say to you, there are some standing here who will not taste death before they see that the kingdom of God has come with power." (Mark 8:27—9:1)

In my English *Gospel Parallels,* Mark 8:27–33 (Peter's confession proper) is one division or section, and 8:34—9:1 (called "the conditions of discipleship") is another.[1] Aland's Greek *Synopsis* divides the same amount of text into three parts: 8:27–30 ("Peter's confession"); 8:31–33 ("Jesus foretells his passion"); and 8:34—9:1 ("If any man would come after me . . .").[2] These divisions of the text are thoroughly understandable and justifiable as marking off apparent changes in the subject matter. In fact, the three sections of Aland's division may represent three traditional units. We shall come around to that question in due course. Yet if one looks at the Gospel of Mark as a literary document, as a narrative, it is clear that the scene that is laid in Mark 8:27 ends only at 9:1. In 8:27 we are told that Jesus "went on with his disciples, to the villages of Caesarea Philippi." (Is the setting on Gentile soil significant for Mark? Quite possibly so, in view of his understanding of the gospel mission.) On the way, he put the question "Who do men say that I am?"—which led to Peter's confession. In Mark 9:2 the separate transfiguration scene is introduced with the phrase "and after six days." (We are told nothing of what happened in the six intervening days.) Clearly Mark 8:27—9:1 constitutes a single episode in the narrative, and on that basis alone, although there are other reasons, we are justified in treating it as a separate and complete unit. (This is the Gospel lection for the Seventeenth Sunday after Pentecost of Year B. The ecumenical lectionaries do not divide the text in this way; some read Mark 8:27–35, others 8:27–38.)

A cursory examination is sufficient to show that there are other reasons for regarding Mark 8:27—9:1 as a unity. The questions of Jesus to his disciples evoke Peter's response, "You are the Christ." Jesus then enjoins the disciples to secrecy about it. This injunction to secrecy is typical of Mark: when the demons recognize Jesus he silences them; when Jesus heals people he frequently tells them to be quiet about it. Now the confession of Peter evokes Jesus' command of silence. Why? We stay now strictly at the level of the narrative, without raising questions about historicity or the shape, formation, and transmission of the tradition. Why, then, the command to silence? Look ahead. Immediately there follows the first passion prediction. Jesus predicts his own coming suffering, rejection, death, and resurrection (Mark 8:31). Mark underscores the fact that Jesus has said this plainly (8:32a). But immediately, Peter begins to rebuke Jesus. Apparently he does not notice that Jesus has predicted his resurrection as well as his rejection, suffering, and death. Jesus then, "turning and seeing his disciples," rebukes Peter, "Get behind me, Satan!" Peter's inability to accept the teaching about Jesus' destiny of death appears to be related to Jesus' earlier admonition to keep silent about his messiahship. It is as if Jesus sensed that Peter's confession of him as Christ was based on false, or at least faulty, premises. That this was in fact the case comes to light when Peter reacts against Jesus' prediction of his passion. "You are not on the side of God, but of man," Jesus tells him. At the point of this rebuke Peter has fallen from the heights—seemingly attained when he gave the christologically correct answer to Jesus' question—to the depths of rejection.

Jesus does not necessarily leave Peter at the bottom of the well, but Peter now recedes completely into the background. Jesus calls to him the multitude—which quite suddenly appears as if from nowhere—and the disciples and begins to speak to them. He invites anyone who would be a disciple, whether from the multitude or from the Twelve, to deny himself, take up his cross, and follow him (Mark 8:34). Next come the sayings about saving one's life and losing it (8:35–37). Then there is the ominous saying in which Jesus relates anyone's rejection of himself in the present to the Son of man's rejection of that person in the final judgment (8:38). With this saying, matters are put into an eschatological perspective typical of Mark. Then it is not surprising that the conclusion is the saying about some standing there "who will not taste death before they see the kingdom of God come with power" (9:1). We may well ask what has happened to Peter. We are not told specifically; indeed, he is not mentioned again. Yet in the very next scene, the Transfiguration, Peter is with Jesus again, along with James and John. Again Peter does not come off very well (". . . he did not know what to say . . ."). Yet there is no indication of his permanent rejection. As we all know, it is one of the features of the Gospel story that Peter keeps bouncing back, by the grace and forgiveness of the Lord.

Up to this point we have not been doing redaction criticism in the stricter sense. Redaction criticism as it is generally construed presupposes the separation of tradition and redaction and the possibility of distinguishing them in the text. We have, however, been attempting to appreciate the movement and meaning of the Marcan narrative as it is given us. That is redaction criticism in the broader sense, of composition criticism. As we now turn to the question of the identification of tradition—no simple task—we would do well to make some observations about the problems this text presents as a historical narrative, for that is what it purports to be.

According to Vincent Taylor's form-critical classification, it is a story about Jesus; Dibelius thinks Mark 8:27–30 has not yet become a legend but that the Matthean counterpart (Matt. 16:13–20) has attained that status; Bultmann places the Marcan account among the legends but thinks it is truncated.[3] The original form of the legend is to be found in Matthew, where Peter's correct response, "You are the Christ, the Son of the living God," is properly celebrated (Matt. 16:17–19). Bultmann believes the primary setting of the confession was the Aramaic-speaking Palestinian church, which venerated Peter, and that the whole account was originally a resurrection story. Now the fat is in the fire. Bultmann's belief that we are here dealing with a resurrection story is wedded to his view that Jesus in his historical ministry did not claim to be the Messiah. Peter was, however, the first to recognize him as such, not during his earthly ministry but only when he saw the risen Jesus. At that point Peter confessed him as Messiah. The accolades Jesus then bestowed on Peter are commensurate with the importance of the occasion. At the point where Peter sees the risen Jesus and confesses him to be the Christ, Christian faith, properly speaking, begins. (It is also at that point that Simon receives the sobriquet "Peter," "Rock.") Once one begins to think as Bultmann does, his proposal does not seem farfetched. Moreover, it does supply a lacuna in the earliest history of the church. Peter was the first to see the risen Jesus (1 Cor. 15:5; Luke 24:34). We have, however, no account of that event unless this is it. What Bultmann takes from us, historically speaking, with one hand, he gives back with the other. He takes away a central scene from Jesus' ministry, but in its place he puts a resurrection scene.

All this may be very interesting to the preacher, as well as to the New Testament scholar and theologian, but what will a congregation make of it? A fair question, but we need to remind ourselves that this is not necessarily to be preached, although it is in the service of preaching. Whatever else preachers may do, if they are really to preach from a Gospel, any New Testament Gospel, they must inform themselves about the text. To do this means, among other things, to become informed about the origin and historical roots of the text. There is a serious question as to whether this text is rooted in an event of Jesus' earthly ministry or in an encounter with the risen Lord.

Having conceded that, one would also want to say that it is by no means certain that we are *not* here dealing with an event of Jesus' Galilean ministry. Yet even if this is the case, there are some problems in taking the story as it stands as an account of what actually happened. For one thing, the inability of Peter and the disciples to understand Jesus' passion predictions, though he tells them plainly, is a recurrent theme of Mark's Gospel. Later on it is the disciples as a group who do not understand (Mark 9:32). Still later, when Jesus is arrested, the disciples flee in panic. In the accounts of the other Gospels the resurrection comes as a surprise to the disciples. Yet according to Mark, Jesus has repeatedly told the disciples not only that he would be killed but also that after three days he would rise from the dead (8:31; 9:31; 10:34; cf. 9:9–10). These passion predictions are quite similar and apparently stereotyped in each of their three occurrences. Jesus says approximately the same thing each time. In no case is there indication that the disciples understand. In fact, in each case it is clear that they do not, for the passion predictions are followed either by an outright protest (Mark 8:32) or by patent examples of the disciples' failure to understand and appropriate the message of Jesus (9:33ff.; 10:35ff.). In this repetition, with its thematic emphasis on the disciples' failure to understand, we see the hand of the evangelist at work.

Moreover, there is reason to think that Mark 8:27—9:1 has been composed out of pieces of tradition which were originally independent but which have been assembled here with a purpose, whether by Mark or by his predecessors. The repetition of the passion predictions (8:31) may already be an indication of this. The saying about cross-bearing (8:34) has an apparent Q-parallel (Matt. 10:38–39; Luke 14:27), as do the sayings about the relation of confessing Jesus now and the final judgment (Mark 8:38; cf. Matt. 10:33; Luke 12:9). In other words, both Matthew and Luke have a parallel to these sayings in a Marcan context, where they are presumably following Mark, and a Q-parallel (one common to Matthew and Luke only) in a different context. This is strong evidence that the sayings in question did not originally belong together here but circulated independently. Most likely, Mark or his predecessors put them together in the aftermath of the confession of Peter and the passion prediction.

The identification of purely Marcan redactional material is difficult, but there are several traces of Mark's hand. At the conclusion of the confession proper comes Jesus' admonition to silence (Mark 8:30), a typical Marcan motif. The next saying, the stereotyped passion prediction (8:31), is introduced by the phrase "and he began to teach them." The use of the verb "begin" with the infinitive of another verb ("to teach") is typical of Mark, as is the verb "to teach" itself, along with the noun "teaching." (Mark emphasizes Jesus' teaching role, although he does not relate his teachings.) Again, in introducing Peter's response, Mark says (8:32), "And Peter took him, and began to rebuke him." After the interchange with Peter, the set of Jesus' sayings which follows (8:34ff.) is introduced by the conventional phrase "And he called to him the multitude with his disciples, and said to them. . . ." As we have already noted, most of these sayings were transmitted independently. The final saying, Mark 9:1, which seems to explain the eschatological standpoint of the Marcan church, is also introduced—unnecessarily— by a typical Marcan formula, "and he said to them."

Thus many signs point to a deliberate arrangement of traditional material, very likely the work of Mark, in which the confession of Peter is first interpreted by the passion prediction; that is, Jesus' messiahship means suffering and death. Then, in turn, the suffering and death of Jesus are, by the sayings of Jesus taken from tradition, related to discipleship (Mark 8:34ff.). Being a disciple of Jesus means to follow him, even in suffering and death. Whether or not one is faithful in this, that is, whether or not one is ashamed of Jesus, is a matter for the weightiest, final judgment. The importance of understanding Jesus' messiahship and the way to which he calls his disciples is underscored by this eschatological sanction.

The fact that we are dealing with Mark's composition does not, however, mean that Mark or the early church simply invented the whole scene. Nor does the fact that separate pieces of tradition are invoked to interpret the confession of Peter mean that they do not bring to expression a historically as well as theologically true interpretation of the meaning, and even the intention, of Jesus' ministry. One can also make a case for the historicity of the confession as an event within Jesus' earthly ministry. Conceivably Mark has cut a traditional story short in order to get at what in his judgment is its real meaning, the teaching about messiahship and discipleship. Bultmann, who admittedly thought the confession was a resurrection legend, proposed that a more primitive form of the story is found in Matthew, where Jesus gives Peter an accolade for recognizing him as the Messiah and vests him with the power of the keys. The scene therefore comes to a more satisfactory and fulfilling conclusion. This is appropriate for a resurrection story, but what if the story had its inception in an actual event of Jesus' public ministry? The very inconclusiveness of the Marcan form lends it a certain verisimilitude. One may even ask whether the question of Jesus which sets things in motion was a genuine one.[4] Jesus seeks his proper role. Peter affirms him as Messiah. Jesus reacts with ambivalence. Mark and the later church, looking at the event from the standpoint of its outcome, particularly the cross, interpret the ambivalence as an expression of Jesus' own knowledge of his coming death and his interpretation of its meaning for himself and his followers. This is a possible historical scenario, but it is nevertheless conjectural, if not speculative. One would rightly hesitate to preach on such a basis.

Turning back to the matter of preaching, we may now ask what the preacher should do with such an analysis of the pericope as we have just sketched. Although an exact and thorough separation of Marcan redaction from traditional material has not been and probably cannot be carried through, the drift or direction of what Mark has done has become increasingly clear. Also, the probable background against which Mark is working has come to light. Mark addresses a church all too confident of Jesus' power and messiahship. He does not present the confession of Peter that Jesus is Messiah as something unknown to the reader. Rather, he seems to assume that the intended reader will know and agree with that affirmation. (In the very beginning of the Gospel, Jesus is said to be Son of God. Then, later on, demons confess his supernatural power.) Mark addresses a Christian audience. The readers, therefore, stand, or can stand, where Peter stands in the sense that they have already confessed that Jesus is the Messiah. Naturally, Mark agrees with that confession; indeed, he regards it as indispensable. Yet that confession per se is not Mark's point. It is not in itself the culmination toward which he is striving. The way Mark has constructed this scene reveals that he works from as well as toward the confession at this stage of the narrative. That is, he takes for granted the appropriateness of the confession and asks what now needs to be understood because of it. What does the confession mean? Not what does it mean for the historical Jesus, but what does it imply for those who confess and follow him? Thus the discussion moves very quickly—with a demand for silence which underscores the dangerous possibility of misunderstanding—from the confession to its consequences and implications. The consequence for Jesus is his role of suffering Son of man. The consequence for his followers is that they as disciples are called upon to suffer. Thus the theme of discipleship gives focus and direction to the scene as Mark constructs and construes it.

Preachers who attend to this text would do well to accept the foothold Mark offers them. Mark does not put the disciple where Peter was *before* the first Caesarea Philippi. Mark does not ask the reader to decide whether Jesus is the Christ; the reader has already decided that question as Peter had decided it. Rather, Mark confronts readers who have already decided and challenges them to accept the way of discipleship which unfolds from the concept of messiahship Jesus embraces. That kind of messiahship is not what Peter expected, and it may not be the kind of messiahship and discipleship that the readers, steeped in the miracle tradition, want to affirm and celebrate. But Mark challenges them to realize in their own life the true discipleship that Jesus commands.

If this insight is correct, what does it mean for preaching from this text? For one thing, the sermon that is so often preached from the confession narrative—I mean the obvious one about the recognition and confession of Jesus as the Christ—is not the sermon that is in closest accord with Mark's narrative. In Mark the confession is integrally bound up with and interpreted by the predictions of the passion and the sayings about discipleship as following Jesus in the way of the cross. Mark does not address outsiders and challenge them to accept Christ. He addresses converts who are already a part of the church and challenges them to accept the suffering of the Son of man for themselves.

Conceivably, the story of the confession of Peter, if traditional, had its original postresurrection *Sitz* and function in the missionary preaching of the gospel. It still conveys the sense of confrontation and challenge that it had in that setting. Yet it has been adapted by Mark to the situation of the church. That is, a story that may originally have been used in missionary preaching has been adapted by Mark for the church's preaching. Mark would have changed its focus and direction so that it now speaks to the church, to people who have already confessed Jesus as Christ. Thus Mark has directed it to a church situation analogous to our own. (Naturally, there are vast differences of time and place.) It is ironic that so often in preaching from the confession of Peter we ignore the way Mark has interpreted it and go back to the setting of the story in the church's missionary preaching or in the ministry of Jesus. When that is done, the Christian congregation is addressed as if it did not believe that Jesus is the Christ. Thus it is not viewed as the church at all—the church which in Matthew's version is built upon the confession that Jesus is the Christ. Instead, the people of the congregation are treated as if their previous professions of faith are defunct, and they are asked to stand where Peter stood before his confession. They are asked to profess faith in Jesus, or to renew a faith in Jesus that must be presumed to have become defunct. For a Christian congregation this is psychologically as well as historically impossible, and Mark's particular emphasis on the interrelationship of messiahship and discipleship is lost.

I have been careful not to say that if a sermon based on this text calls for a decision for Christ it is illegitimate. It is not, but at best it is truncated and will probably miss Mark's point. To be legitimate the confession of Jesus as Christ must be the confession that Jesus the suffering Son of man is the Christ. The messianic role of Jesus is misunderstood if it is not understood in this way. But Mark is not primarily interested in evoking the messianic confession per se. He assumes it. Thus Mark gives definite guidance on how to preach and what to preach, on the basis of this narrative of Peter's confession. Why not take a cue from Mark?

One might ask, "Does that not mean to preach Mark instead of Jesus?" But Christian faith is not faith in Jesus of Nazareth, in the sense that we might hope to leapfrog over nearly two thousand years of history to lay hold of Jesus himself. To believe in Jesus is to believe that the New Testament interpretation of him is true. It is to believe that the preaching of Mark is authentic preaching of Jesus, that preaching from Mark is authentic preaching of Jesus. Therefore, there are good theological grounds to reject the dilemma of Mark or Jesus.

It belongs to the genius of Mark (or of the early church which produced Mark) that his Gospel narrative moves on at least three levels, or allows for three levels of interpretation. There is first of all the level of the narrative itself, on which Jesus addresses his disciples (and others). This level had and has its distinct, historical reality. There is also the analogous level of Mark the evangelist addressing his church or audience. In and behind the figures of Jesus and the disciples we perceive Mark and the Marcan church. (Conversely, Mark and the Marcan church are in the picture only because of what has transpired between Jesus and his disciples. That is, the latter are not the creation of Mark; Mark is unthinkable apart from them.) As Jesus addressed his disciples, so Mark addresses the church of his time. For the contemporary reader or hearer and preacher there is yet another level.[5] Today's preacher and congregation have an invitation and a right to stand where Mark and his congregation or readers stood. So, as Mark addressed his church, preachers may also address their congregations. The preacher stands where Mark stands, who stands where Jesus stood. The responsibility is awesome! The possibilities for perverting and misconstruing this authority are real, just as the possibilities for perverting and misconstruing the messianic authority of Jesus were real. But who authorizes the preacher to speak if not the New Testament evangelist, and who authorizes the evangelist to speak, if not Jesus? We preachers do not, of course, assume the prerogatives of Jesus, or even of the evangelist. We simply convey their word. So for the preacher to enter into this relationship is not presumptuous. Indeed, the presumption is to presume to preach without standing in this relationship to the text, to its author, and to Jesus.

5

PREACHING FROM MATTHEW

THE MARCAN TEXT we have been examining might well become the basis for many different sermons. There is a sense in which that is true of any Gospel text, any biblical text for that matter. There are as many sermons as there are situations or preachers. Yet it is particularly true of Mark's rendition of the confession of Peter, for that text is fundamental to Mark and to Mark's understanding of the meaning of Jesus and the gospel. It is a central or key text, that is, everything else either proceeds from it or is implicit in it. Indeed, preaching from other Marcan texts not only may be but should be influenced by an understanding or interpretation of it.

We now look at two other synoptic texts to illustrate how they may be appropriated in preaching. One is from Matthew, the other from Luke. Both were assigned or given to me, in the sense that they are lectionary texts; both actually became the basis for sermons. For weal or woe, the sermons I preached are reproduced here. These particular sermons have been selected for several reasons. For one thing, they are not on Mark, and it will be helpful to ask how one goes about preaching from the other synoptic Gospels. These sermons may also provide some insight into the character of Matthew and Luke. Moreover, these two Gospel texts relate to Mark in different ways. Matthew has been described as an expanded version of the Gospel of Mark. While such a characterization scarcely does justice to the evangelist's achievement, there is some truth in it. That should come to light in the sermon based on the Matthean version of the parable of the sower, which in turn is based on the Marcan rendition of that parable. A basic redaction-critical procedure in interpreting Matthew or Luke is to compare their renditions with the Marcan parallel wherever the latter is available. On the other hand, the sermon on the Lucan Annunciation deals with a text that is in no way drawn from or directly related to the Gospel of Mark. Luke is here going his independent way, although there are some significant points of contact with Matthew's infancy story. In the one case, a relationship to Mark needs to be taken into account; in the other, there is no such relationship, and one must rather ask how and why the evangelist does what he does.

Both sermons were preached in Duke University Chapel. The congregation there, which varies considerably in composition from Sunday to Sunday, may be more liberal and intellectually sophisticated than average. I firmly believe, however, that no greater mistake can be made in such a setting than to try to preach an "intellectual" sermon. The congregation, like all Christian congregations, may be presumed to consist mainly of Christians in need of inspiration, encouragement, and reassurance, as well as stimulation, challenge, and prodding. The typical error is to underestimate what the congregation is capable of hearing. In the university setting the danger is to overestimate, or wrongly estimate, it.

The structure of the sermon on Matthew[1] (indeed, of both sermons) is very simple: what my homiletics teacher, James T. Cleland, called an "Old Expository I," consisting basically of exegesis, exposition, and application.[2] An ironclad theoretical distinction between exegesis and exposition is not really defensible. Indeed, if one thinks of a hermeneutical circle or, better, ellipse, in which the word of God (represented by a biblical text) and a specific human situation are brought into relation to one another, it becomes impossible to regard any of the three aspects or elements of the sermon as separate and distinct from the other. For example, the perception of a need for a distinctly Christian kind of understanding in the university community (application) did not simply arise out of this text. It influenced what I saw in the text. Such an influence of one's own situation and perception upon exegesis is wrong exegetically only when it causes one to see in the text what is not there.

THE PARABLE OF THE SOWER: A SERMON ON MATTHEW 13:1–23

Introduction

The Gospel lesson for this morning is Matthew's rendition of the parable of the sower. Jesus might have become a little amused—I hope not outraged—at the spectacle of preachers expounding his parables. But the preacher who does it is in good company. Matthew himself was no earlier than the second, quite likely the third or fourth, preacher to expound and interpret the parable of the sower. Mark preceded him. In all probability a tradition of interpretation or preaching antedated Mark. Yet at best there is something faintly ludicrous about explaining Jesus' parables. It would seem that the parable itself is intended to make something clear. If it is not entirely explicit in its message, that very quality contributes to its character as parable. Presumably, Jesus had some purpose in putting his message into parabolic form, he did it so often.

Not long ago, I read a book on the uses of structuralism in biblical exegesis or interpretation. (Those of you familiar with structuralism will know what that is about; those of you who are not would scarcely profit from my explanation of it.) After a learned exposition of several leading exponents of structuralist method and thought, the author set about to demonstrate it by applying it to the parable of the good Samaritan. I read the author's erudite discussion with amazement, but then I wondered whether it might be for me another sophisticated way of leaving the man attacked by robbers in the ditch. I had read and heard Jesus' parable and thought I had understood enough to be disquieted. Now I felt myself being led down paths of restful confusion through valleys of amazed perplexity. One recalls Karl Barth's alleged dictum, uttered in another connection, that God did not intend for us first to learn Chinese in order to understand the gospel. (And I suppose God also didn't intend for the Chinese to have to learn English either.) Or there is Halford Luccock, late professor of preaching at Yale Divinity School, who emerged from a lecture on revelation by his distinguished colleague H. Richard Niebuhr. Not much had been revealed to him. "I am thankful," muttered Luccock, "that the Lord said feed my sheep, not feed my giraffes." In other words, it suffices to put the cookies on a lower shelf.

We have an innate sense that the gospel of Jesus is simple enough to be understood by simple people, and we are surely not wrong in that.

Transition

One reason we think this way is the presence in the New Testament, especially in the Gospels, of so many parables of Jesus. Here are brief and simple stories, told in the language of a predominantly rural society, stories which do not seem to put too great a strain on the hearers' or readers' intellectual capacity. For centuries, at least until the emergence of modern industrial and technological society, these parables spoke an almost universal language of seedtime and harvest, the shared experiences of people who lived close to nature and the land. "Tell me the stories, of Jesus, I love to hear." We expect to hear something familiar. In fact, most people who down through the centuries have heard Jesus' parables have heard something familiar.

1. EXEGESIS

Perhaps there is no more familiar parable than that of the sower, which we just heard read. Of course, you all listened attentively while that Gospel lesson was read. But just because the sermon topic was announced as the parable of the sower does not mean that someone is actually going to address himself to that text. Moreover, what is familiar can become too familiar, and we do not even hear it. So perhaps we would do well to remind ourselves of what we are talking about. Our text falls into three parts: (1) the parable itself; (2) the disciples' question and Jesus' statement about the purpose of parables generally; (3) the explanation of the parable of the sower.

Matthew tells us Jesus was so pressed by the crowds along the lakeshore that he got into a boat and addressed the crowd from there. Jesus spoke to the crowd in parables, and Matthew relates this parable, presumably as a specimen of what Jesus said. A sower sows seed which fall in different places: along the path, where birds devour it; on rocky ground, where it is soon scorched by the sun; on thorns, where it is soon choked out. Yet some does fall on good soil and bears fruit (or grain), a hundredfold, sixtyfold, and thirtyfold. "He who has ears to hear, let him hear," says Jesus.

Now if we were not told that this was a parable of Jesus, and also, later on in this text, what its interpretation might be, our reaction might not be entirely positive. "Far out!" we might think, or, "Off the wall." Or, more than likely, "So what?" Even the importance of the subject, the harvest, does not seem so urgent to us—at least not until we encounter yet another round of price increases at the supermarket or see farmers on TV declaiming their determination not to plant again unless they get better prices. We do not feel the urgency of the issues involved in the imagery. Of course, we are right in sensing that the parable is not about agriculture, but farming provides imagery that is appropriate, for what is at stake, Jesus seems to imply, is no less a life-and-death matter than the success of the harvest.

Still the meaning of the parable is not obvious, not such a simple matter. Matthew apparently here follows one of his sources, the Gospel of Mark, and next portrays the disciples asking Jesus why he speaks to the crowds in parables. Their question reflects a perplexity which any hearer or reader might feel at this point. Jesus gives them a rather long answer. He seems to be saying that what is plain to the disciples must be stated in parables to the multitudes. It is not clear to me whether the parables are to help the crowds understand or whether Jesus' speech seems parabolic to them just because they don't understand. A very difficult passage, but Matthew is not as difficult as Mark.

In Mark, Jesus says quite explicitly that he speaks to those outside, nondisciples, in parables *so that* they will not understand and be forgiven. That was too much for Matthew, who evidently thought that our Lord could not have said such a thing. So Matthew changes the wording just enough that Jesus does not say that. *Then* Matthew quotes Isaiah more fully to the effect that unbelief is the fulfillment of Scripture. Whatever his reasons or grounds for departing from Mark, Matthew was in all probability right historically in refusing to represent Jesus' parables as a means of obfuscation, indeed condemnation.

After what amounts to a softening of Mark's harsh parable theory, Matthew gives Jesus' interpretation of the parable of the sower. The seed falling upon the various soils are equated with different hearers of the word. Finally, the seed sown in good soil are those people who hear and understand the word and bring forth fruit. It all sounds so obvious now, but in all probability, even this is some early preacher's interpretation of what Jesus meant. Seldom in the Gospels does Jesus offer such an interpretation of his parables. The parable of the sower appears in the apocryphal Gospel of Thomas without interpretation. (Probably the parable first circulated without it.) Also the language, the technical terminology of the interpretation, reflects the situation of the early church. For example, "the word" here means the Christian gospel. Accordingly, the parable is about the success of the gospel among those who at first accept it. Elsewhere Jesus does not speak in this way. Probably we are here witness to the earliest interpretation of one of Jesus' parables. The first Christians understood the parable in relation to their own situation, and that was not such a bad, or a wrong, idea. Yet Jesus naturally spoke this parable with his own situation in view. As the messenger who announces the reality and coming of God's kingdom, his rule, Jesus himself is the sower who goes forth to sow. His preaching and his ministry find different receptions among different people. A lot of people react positively; he gets an enthusiastic reception. Yet many more wither in the heat of the day than endure or persist.

Reading the Gospel of Matthew is, as we now see, like looking through a kaleidoscope or peeling an onion. One can distinguish what Matthew added to Mark, what Mark wrote, what Mark got from the early church's preaching, and what Jesus himself said. There are layers of meaning, but there is no reason to doubt that Jesus uttered this parable. It is also as certain as can be that Jesus wanted to say something about the kingdom or rule of God. All the Gospels, Matthew particularly, put the parable of the sower at the head of a group of parables of the kingdom. In doing so they preserve the original intention of the parable. Moreover, as I read Matthew I do not see only competing or conflicting meanings. There is a unity in what is said, even if it is said by more than one witness. Furthermore—and I want to underscore this—Matthew puts his finger on an important thread that runs through the text and runs from the text back to Jesus himself. In the interpretation of the parable, only Matthew writes (Matt. 13:19), "When any one hears the word of the kingdom and does not understand it"—understand it!—"the evil one comes and snatches away what is sown in his heart." At the end of the interpretation (v. 23) he writes that he who hears the word and understands it bears fruit. Only Matthew speaks positively of the disciples' understanding. At the end of the parable collection (v. 51) in Matthew, and Matthew only, Jesus asks his disciples, "Have you understood all this?" They answer, "Yes."

Transition

There is no doubt that we have uncovered an important and distinctive motif of Matthew's Gospel. Christian discipleship according to Matthew is not only obeying Jesus but also understanding him. But is there more to it than this?

2. EXPOSITION

Yes, there is. Matthew is pointing to something ingredient to, essential to, being Christian, being a disciple of Jesus. Let's take a few moments to look at the ways in which Matthew's emphasis on understanding really makes sense of the parable, that is, makes sense of what Jesus said and makes sense of Jesus' habit of speaking in parables.

Jesus did not appear on the scene discussing theology or even debating questions about the interpretation of the law. He announced the advent of God's kingdom. He spoke in hyperbole—or so it seems—about turning the other cheek and going the extra mile. He spoke in parables in answer to questions or in order to make a point about God's kingdom or rule. In fact, in the Gospels, Jesus never answers or speaks directly to the question "What is the kingdom of God?" Jesus seems to assume his hearers will understand what he means by "kingdom of God." Yet it is not altogether clear that all his Jewish contemporaries would have understood the same thing by that phrase. Jesus' language is suggestive, evocative. His parables elicit understanding on the part of his hearers. The question that his parables pose for the hearer is Do you grasp what I'm talking about?

The answer is not a matter of purely intellectual assent. With Jesus it has to do with the nearness of God's rule. With the earliest church it has to do with the good news that God's rule is present in Jesus. Then it becomes a question whether people will accept it. Matthew makes it explicit that this is a question of understanding. But in either case the question implicit in the parable of the sower is what one makes of Jesus himself. Do you understand who I am? what I am doing? why I am here? But that question is never a silly, irrelevant, abstract, or pointless question. The question about Jesus is not just an otherworldly question. It is put to the disciples, and to the church, where they are. It is asked not in the cloister but in the world of people and events. The sower went forth to sow. He scatters seed among all sorts and conditions of people. He comes saying the reign of God is at hand, his kingdom is near. Is this rather strange itinerant preacher, who casts out demons, heals the sick, and associates with undesirables, somehow the token and embodiment of God's rule? Does he have a right to make demands of me? In fact, he does so. But his demand is at the same time a question. Thus he speaks in parables. "A sower went out to sow." Do you know what's happening? "A man was going down from Jerusalem to Jericho." "Which of these three, do you think, proved neighbor to the man who fell among robbers?"

Transition

Jesus' speaking in parables is itself a challenge to understand. Believing and obeying are, of course, essential. But a meaningful obedience of faith requires understanding. To be disciples of Jesus we must know not only who he is and where he is but who we are and where we are. Jesus' probing parables call forth a response, not intellectual sophistication but what we might call moral and spiritual insight. Matthew rightly speaks of understanding. The simplest person is capable of it. The most sophisticated intellectual may miss the point.

3. APPLICATION

Several years ago I was observing a divinity student leading a discussion in a youth group at a church not far from here. We might describe it as a "working class" church. The subject of the discussion was communism. The discussion was going rather badly. The young person doing most of the talking apparently had some canned material from "Lifeline" or a similar source. Eventually the talk got around to school integration, Duke student demonstrations, and matters closer home. As it did it got better. The young people could understand their parents' strong feelings but thought the parents intolerant. Finally, the girl who had been reading the anti-communist propaganda had a flash of insight. "As Christians," she said, "we should love everybody. We must love communists and black people and Duke people." I stifled a laugh, and for years I have told this story in a condescending way. It seemed to illustrate so marvelously the way in which many people in town regard Duke University and "Duke people."

But now I have second thoughts. This young person had a perfectly valid and important Christian insight. It came home, especially as far as black people and Duke people were concerned, to where she was. (I might add parenthetically that as years have passed I have found that loving Duke people is not such an inconsiderable challenge after all!) As members of an academic community we can be insufferably self-assured and self-righteous. But such learning and prestige as we possess is no guarantee we have the kind of insight and understanding which Jesus demands. Indeed, we do not always agree and are not always right. William F. Buckley once said he would rather be governed by the first one thousand people in the Boston telephone book than by the faculty of Harvard University. I'm uncertain whether I'd want to apply that to Durham and Duke, but be that as it may, the longer I reflect the more I rejoice in a young girl's spontaneous insight that the gospel lays upon her the demand to love her neighbors, even if they are Duke people. And it occurs to me to think that the reverse of that is also true for us. We who are members of an academic community, for all our penchant for self-criticism and debate, find it easy to esteem and in a real sense love our colleagues. We find it much less easy to esteem and to love those who do not share our intellectual and related commitments. But whom we do not esteem as equal before God we can scarcely love.

For those of us who would live at once in the university and in the church of Jesus Christ, there may be a painful but necessary acknowledgment. True, the values and goals of the two in many ways overlap and are mutually supportive. The goals of the university are valid and valuable; I do not for a moment disparage them. Yet the understanding which, according to the New Testament, Jesus calls for is not the same as the understanding we seek in the university. That distinctively Christian understanding is based not upon erudition but upon an insight born of faith. It is available not to the arrogant and haughty but to the lowly and to people who have put all pretense aside.

Whoever can hear and understand the parables of Jesus will gain this saving knowledge. So, at the conclusion of the parable of the sower, Jesus says, "He who has ears, let him hear." So be it. May we hear indeed. Amen.

This sermon is somewhat unusual in that it contains so much explicit exegesis. In this respect it should not be taken as a model. Yet the text is interesting, and the comparison with its Marcan source leads into questions of the origin, form, and history of the parable. Thus it is possible to speak of a form history *(Formgeschichte)* of the parable in a quite specific and literal sense. Certainly following such a sermon as this asks something of the congregation. One of my colleagues asked me whether I thought the congregation understood the exegesis. Since I could not give a pop quiz after the service, it was impossible to say that all did. Judging from comments I heard, some did. In my view, the sermon is not difficult in the sense of being too technical and complex. I have sought to avoid unnecessary complexity as well as the jargon of the scholar. Probably it demands more than many sermons, but that does not in itself mean it demands too much. Perhaps preachers underestimate the congregation more than they overestimate it, preaching too much to the lowest common denominator or to the person with the shortest attention span. Maybe we tell too many stories, at best to drive home a point, at worst to amuse. Here we take a story, as Jesus told it, as Matthew tells it, noting also how Mark told it. We allow ourselves the opportunity to examine that story and to reflect on it. Evidently, this way of preaching from this text interested, and reached, some people. Maybe that is enough.

Several dimensions of criticism are readily apparent in the sermon. I saw no reason to challenge or even question the historicity of the parable. The burden of proof lies on the one who would challenge its authenticity. What is said about its original setting in Jesus' proclamation of the kingdom of God relies heavily on the excellent form-critical work of Jeremias *(The Parables of Jesus)*. The sermonic focus is not, however, upon the probable meaning of the parable in the preaching of Jesus, as Jeremias is able to uncover it, although it might have been. At this point we may pause to observe that nothing I have said is intended to rule out preaching on a word or deed of Jesus in the context of Jesus' own message and mission. The point is that such preaching ought to be critically informed and to proceed circumspectly. It is not best done by recklessly throwing caution to the winds and wildly exercising an uninhibited imagination.

This sermon's point really emerges from a comparison of the Matthean and Marcan versions of the parable. What seemed to me most worth underscoring was Matthew's emphasis on understanding. In the conclusion of the interpretation (13:23), Matthew speaks of hearing the word and understanding it, whereas Mark speaks only of hearing and accepting it. Then at the conclusion of the entire parable discourse

Matthew (13:51) alone has Jesus ask the disciples whether they have
understood, and they answer that they have. The theme of the disciples'
understanding is distinctly Matthean. Recent research in the redaction
history of Matthew has shown that the evangelist had a high Christology and put a premium on Jesus' divine sonship.[3] At the same time
Matthew also emphasizes the teaching of Jesus (7:24–29): Jesus, as Son
of God, gives commandments which are to be taught by his disciples as
they in turn make disciples of all nations (Matt. 28:16–20). Unlike
Mark, Matthew and Luke convey a substantial representation of Jesus'
teaching (in the "Q" traditions shared by Matthew and Luke, as well as
in other material distinctive of each, sometimes called "M" and "L").
Matthew's theme of the disciples' understanding then agrees with and
complements his emphasis on Jesus' teaching.

The importance of this theme of understanding might have been even
better brought out in the sermon had I made more of the crowd's not
understanding (Matt. 13:13) and especially Matthew's full citation of
Isa. 6:9–10 (not found in Mark or Luke): "You shall indeed hear but
never understand. . . ." Matthew's invoking of the motif of not understanding through his use of the Isaiah text serves as the foil for his
emphasis upon the disciples' understanding. I might also have noted
that this notion of understanding the parable, which Matthew has
placed at the end of the parable's interpretation, is found at the beginning of the interpretation in Mark (4:13). There Jesus asks the disciples,
almost incredulously, "Do you not understand this parable? How then
will you understand all the parables?" In Mark the prospects for the
disciples' understanding do not look good (despite Mark 4:34, where it
is said that Jesus explained everything to his disciples privately). Neither
at the end of the parable interpretation nor at the end of the parable
collection is the reader reassured that the disciples understood. This fits
Mark's view of the disciples, which stands in some contrast to Matthew's view. In Mark the disciples frequently do not understand; in
Matthew they do. To bring out this contrast further would have underscored the point about the importance of disciples' understanding in
Matthew, but it would have made the exegesis even longer and more
complex. In preaching, when an exegetical point is clear, and clearly
stated, there is no need to prove it conclusively as if one were writing a
scholarly article.

The emphasis in the sermon on Matthew's meaning does not mean

Mark is contradicted or that Jesus himself is regarded as irrelevant. Rather, the sermon focuses upon one aspect of the parable text at one point in its development. That is, it focuses on the concept of understanding as it is brought to the surface in Matthew's version or redaction. The comparison of Matthew with Mark helped me, the preacher, appreciate Matthew's emphasis on understanding. Of course, other sermons could be preached on this or other aspects of the text. A sermon does not distort a text just because it does not deal with every aspect of it. To snatch a text out of context means to ignore, disregard, or contradict the context. One may certainly deal with one aspect of a text and at the same time respect its context. In fact, to deal with every detail of a text will all too often result in an unduly complex sermon if not an utterly boring one.

But what about the relation of Jesus to this text? It is possible to reason that the oral tradition in which the parable was remembered and interpreted is one step away from Jesus. Mark, who first incorporated it into his Gospel, is two steps away. Matthew, who used Mark as his source, is three steps away, unless perhaps he also drew on an early source independent of Mark. Perhaps he did, but there is little evidence for this. Yet even if he did not, and if we must then conceive of three or four stages (Jesus, tradition, Mark, Matthew) with Matthew at the furthest remove from Jesus, it does not follow that Matthew simply imposes something on the parable that was not previously there and is foreign to it. Matthew may bring out or make explicit what is implicit in it.

For one thing, as we have seen, the misunderstanding of the disciples is a major theme of the Gospel of Mark, which is Matthew's source. It would be quite surprising, however, if the disciples of Jesus actually misunderstood him as fully and consistently, with as little reason, as Mark portrays them doing. In all probability Matthew is not entirely wrong historically in portraying the disciples as understanding Jesus. But aside from this general, commonsense consideration, we may well ask whether or in what more specific sense this Matthean portrayal is true. As I attempted to suggest in the sermon, Jesus' parables demand understanding. Jesus did not say directly everything he thought important. He spoke in a parabolic language that called for and called forth sympathetic insight and understanding. I have a colleague who quite unconsciously tends to whisper when he makes a profound or important point. This mannerism is nevertheless an effective mode of fixing the hearer's attention upon what he is saying. The change in tone rivets your attention and elicits your desire to hear and understand. A different but analogous effect was produced by Jesus' parabolic speech. One's attention is riveted. You desire to hear and understand. To understand, you must appropriate the parable, not just to the general human situation but also to the specific situation of Jesus as speaker and yourself as hearer. This must have been how it was when Jesus himself spoke; it continued to be how it was when his parables were repeated by the early Christians and incorporated into Gospels. It continues to be how it is when his parables are read, spoken, or preached, and heard, today.

When Matthew works with the theme of understanding, therefore, he is not imposing upon the parable text something that is not there. He is not introducing a strange or extraneous idea. Rather, he is working with a theme that is actually already present in his source, Mark. But more than that, he is developing a motif ingredient to the style and character of Jesus' own teaching, especially his parables. He is not then taking us away from Jesus, but in his own way he is leading us to Jesus—to the Jesus who is Lord of his church and of ours. But more than that, he is also leading us to the Jesus who lived and walked and spoke in parables in Galilee in A.D. 30. To believe this belongs both to historical insight and to Christian faith.

6

PREACHING FROM LUKE

THE SERMON we shall be discussing here is based upon the Lucan account of the Annunciation. The Annunciation seems at first to be a simple story, but to the conscientious exegete it nevertheless presents problems. To begin with, it prefigures the miraculous conception and birth of Jesus and constitutes, with the Matthean account, one of the two New Testament foundation stories of the venerable Christian doctrine of the virgin birth. Therein lies a theological problem, at least for many people. This problem is not lessened by the existence of stories about miraculous births in the Old Testament and in the literature of the Greco-Roman world. Perhaps there is nothing quite like the New Testament stories of Jesus' birth in Jewish and pagan antiquity, but they nevertheless reflect an ancient rather than modern perspective, and they represent a genre that is at home in a world other than our own.[1]

The text itself presents some complexities. There is, of course, the historical question, whose problematic character we have already indicated. Doubtless the old question—Did it happen?—is too simply and narrowly put when confined to the matter of the virgin birth. Yet the intention of the narrative to speak of an event must not be lost among the difficulties inherent in the character of that event. Luke is a story-teller, by his own rights a historian, and this primal and instinctive perception must not be surrendered to our theological sophistication or lost through our literary analysis. Luke wants to tell his readers—including us—about something that has happened.

Although the goal may be simple, his literary technique is not. Just the question of the relationship of this text to the Old Testament offers material and issues sufficient for a weighty monograph. Extensive parallels to Luke 1:32–33 may be found in 2 Sam. 7:12–16. Strikingly similar birth annunciations occur, for example, in Gen. 18:9–15 and Judg.

13:2–7. The virginal birth (or conception) evokes the Septuagint of Isa. 7:14. The greeting to Mary in Luke 1:28 may be likened to Judg. 5:24. The promise of the conception of a son (Luke 1:31) is not unlike Judg. 13:3 and Gen. 16:11, as well as Isa. 7:14. Quite possibly Luke has by the use of midrashic techniques (a rabbinic method of Scripture interpretation) deliberately modeled his account on these or other Old Testament texts, some of which already had a history of interpretation in the early church.

Moreover, the Lucan Annunciation has striking points of contact with the Matthean Annunciation (Matt. 1:18–25), despite the marked differences which render literary dependence in either direction unlikely. In each case Mary, a virgin, is betrothed to Joseph, who is, we are informed, of Davidic lineage. In each there is an appearance of the angel Gabriel, who announces the conception of a son by the Holy Spirit and says his name shall be Jesus. Moreover, in both Matthew and Luke the birth of Jesus takes place in Bethlehem. Of course, in Matthew the announcement is to Joseph, while in Luke it is to Mary; and otherwise the narrative details are, generally, different. If, however, the similarities are too extensive to be coincidental, while the differences do not admit of direct literary dependence, some common source or tradition must underlie the two accounts. There was in all probability an early tradition regarding Jesus' birth which Luke has taken up and employed to fulfill his purposes.[2]

Probably the structurally parallel account of the annunciation of the birth of John the Baptist to his father Zechariah is largely, if not altogether, the creation of Luke. The coincidences with the annunciation to Mary are too marked to admit easily of any other explanation. But the Lucan Annunciation story itself, while based upon tradition, is in all likelihood the creation of Luke as it lies before us. Luke and Matthew betray many common traits but no common story which would allow us to reconstruct a primitive narrative tradition from a comparison of the texts. Although the quest for a more primitive narrative cannot and need not concern us here, we must take note of the possibility (suggested by critics of as divergent theological perspectives as Vincent Taylor and Rudolf Bultmann)[3] that an earlier version of the Lucan account—or the traditional story—contained no reference to Jesus' virginal conception. In other words, verses 34–35 or 34–37, which speak of the virginal conception, may have been appended redactionally, whether by Luke or another, later editor. If the verses were not there, they would never be missed. The arguments favoring this proposal are, however, offset by the fact that their removal destroys the climactic parallelism with Luke 1:18–20, where Zechariah expresses amazement at the angel's announcement and receives an answer to his question and a confirmatory (if in his case punitive) sign. In other words, the annunciation to Zechariah presupposes the miraculous character of Jesus' birth. If John's birth is to take place miraculously, it is altogether fitting, according to Luke's literary procedure and theological perspective, that Jesus' birth should be accompanied by even more miraculous circumstances. The virginal conception goes back at least to Luke, if not earlier. Its presence also in Matthew probably means it is earlier.

We turn now to the sermon.[4] Afterward we shall have some further reflections about the problems of preaching from this text.

THE ANNUNCIATION: AN ADVENT SERMON ON LUKE 1:26–38

What would you think if an angel told you that you were going to get pregnant? Probably you wouldn't believe him, particularly if you are over fifty, under twelve, or a male. Or you might not believe that you had seen an angel at all. Or perhaps you'd say, "The only fellow in a white coat I'm going to believe is the gynecologist." We don't have a lot to do with angels any more.

Our text is the annunciation to Mary, and Luke intends to tell us about a miracle. There is no question about that. Mary's astonishment—"How shall this be, since I have no husband?"—is more than matched by our own incredulity. It is true after all that Mary, Joseph, and Jesus lived in a world in which demons ascend from below and angels—like Gabriel—come down from heaven. So it may be that Mary was somewhat better prepared to see an angel than we are. But it would be wrong on the basis of this ancient world view to infer that the astounding and miraculous character of the narrative of Jesus' birth is significantly reduced. Indeed, the appearance of the angel already suggests that we are dealing with extraordinary events. For Luke, as for Mary, a great miracle is about to take place. Its magnitude is underlined by the lesser miracle of the birth of an infant son to the aged Zechariah and Elizabeth. Yet Zechariah and Elizabeth are married and living together, if elderly, while Mary is an unmarried virgin. Thus the story of the miraculous circumstances surrounding John's conception and birth serves to highlight the even greater miracle of Jesus' appearance.

Who can hear and believe such stories nowadays? If I told you an angel had spoken to me, you might not speak to me again. We don't want a lot to do with people who talk to angels. Moreover, there are some good reasons for having doubts or questions about this ancient story. In the first place, only Luke and Matthew in the New Testament describe Jesus' birth. Although they agree that Jesus was conceived prior to and apart from human paternity, their infancy stories are quite different. They agree only on a few startling details such as the virginity of Mary. It is also a bit odd that Mary, already betrothed to Joseph, is so surprised at the angel's promise that she shall bear a son. Might she not have assumed that the angel meant "after you and Joseph are safely married"? But Joseph never comes into the picture—except as the one through whom the Davidic ancestry of Jesus is traced. In fact, in the genealogies of both Matthew and Luke the Davidic ancestry of Jesus is through Joseph. At least according to some early Christian belief, Jesus was a direct descendant of David, on the side of Joseph. Yet according to our Lucan narrative, Joseph has nothing to do with Jesus' birth—and Matthew is even more emphatic on this point. We are confronted with an anomaly in the texts.

Christians who read these texts and take such matters seriously will at this juncture usually go in one of two basic directions. Some may begin to consider such possibilities as that Jesus' Davidic ancestry was on the side of Mary and thus Mary and Joseph were themselves remotely kin. The text, however, says nothing about this. They may also suggest that the angel took Mary so completely by surprise that she forgot about Joseph, whom she may never have met even though she was betrothed to him. Betrothal was by parental agreement rather than romantic attachment. Some may attempt to explain discrepancies between Matthew and Luke by recourse to the age-old story of the three blindfolded gentlemen attempting to determine the shape of the elephant by touch alone. (One felt his tusk, another his ears, the third his trunk.) Thus Matthew and Luke know and tell different aspects of the same story. But it is really not the same story; the points of agreement are more theological than narrative. Moreover, the analogy is imperfect; the Gospel writers are not groping after elephants in the dark.

On the other hand, some Christians take the difficulties in these stories to confirm long-entertained suspicions about the accounts of Jesus' birth. They are fine for the ancients, the elderly, and children, but what man or woman of today can take them seriously? We know, as people of antiquity did not, that virgins too do conceive and bear sons. Then there is the appearance of the angel to Mary. Of course, angels trip lightly onto and off the stage in these stories. Whoever wants to take literally the promise of the virginal conception ought also to be prepared to accept the appearance of Gabriel on the same terms. But we don't have much truck with angels any more. Furthermore, there is a wide range of questions, from the doctrine of the Incarnation to a Christian understanding of sexuality, that is simply set in the wrong perspective by these birth narratives. If Jesus was not conceived and born in the normal way, human sexuality is somehow devalued and Christ's oneness with humankind put in question. In other words, God did it wrong!

Both these approaches, the effort to save the historical credibility of the narrative and the dismissal of it on grounds of its incredibility or unsuitability, fail to do justice to the biblical text. The Annunciation story is not intended to provide answers to certain questions, as important as they may be to us. Nor is justice done the story when its defenders or detractors subject it either to cross-examination or to rational explanation. The evangelist is not concerned with the question of how Jesus can be the Son of David through Joseph and yet not Joseph's natural son, although the text appears to say both things. As though oblivious to such questions, Luke later calls Joseph the father of Jesus; the same Joseph is not responsible for Jesus' conception and birth and at the same time is his earthly parent. Nor is Luke concerned with the proper Christian teaching about sex and family, and such a teaching may not be inferred from the text.

The narrative is about a miracle: Jesus' conception and birth. The primary miracle is that Mary shall conceive and bear a son, Jesus, who "will be great, and will be called the Son of the Most High; and the Lord God will give to him the throne of his father David, . . . and of his kingdom there will be no end." That is a pretty big miracle. The miracle of the virginal conception enters in only secondarily, yet enter it does. There is a certain wonder that accompanies every birth, as you well know if you are a parent. But this birth is uniquely wonderful.

Nevertheless, the point is not a biological curiosity but the initiative and purpose of God expressed in the birth of Jesus. Paul writes, "God was in Christ reconciling the world to himself." John says, "God sent the Son into the world"; or, "The Word became flesh and dwelt among us." This is Luke's way of conveying the same truth.

To people like most of us, who live in the twentieth century and who are Christian first of all by birth and tradition, it may seem less offensive or more credible to think that the Word became flesh and dwelt among us than to think that a virgin conceived and bore a son. The noted Roman Catholic New Testament scholar, Father Raymond Brown, gets to the theological point when he remarks that Christians as a rule believe in the virgin birth (or virginal conception) because they believe Jesus Christ was the Son of God; they do not believe that he was the Christ or God's son simply because he was born of a virgin.[5] That Jesus was born of the virgin is reported in the Koran and presumably believed by Muslims. Yet they do not believe that Jesus was the Son of God in the sense that Christians affirm that he is. So you can believe that Jesus was born under very unusual circumstances without believing what Christians have believed about him.

Some of you may feel that the next step, and the logical one, is to say that the virgin birth is not, after all, so important, or that if one believes that Jesus is the Christ it does not make any difference whether one believes in angels, the virgin birth, and so forth. If you want to draw that conclusion, all right. But before we make that move we ought to reflect a little on what we are assuming.

Is it actually easier to believe that God in that Nazarene carpenter was reconciling the world to himself? If one wants to believe in a miracle, there's one. Is it really less offensive to the assumptions and tastes of modern people that God chose to make himself known through a rejected son of a persecuted people? Is it not astonishing to us that God should reveal himself in poverty, defeat, and death, when we all take for granted that wealth, victory, and life—especially youth—are infinitely more desirable? Is this Jesus the one who will be great, Son of the Most High, king over Israel forever? All natural and ordinary notions of greatness, divine sonship, and kingship are called into question.

Yet Luke does not intend in the Annunciation story to underscore the paradoxical dimension of God's revealing himself in Jesus; that is, he does not emphasize God's revealing his glory in humility and death. Instead, he wants to celebrate the momentous truth that God has, at length, visited his people. Long years of barrenness and oppression are at an end. There is cause for joy and celebration. Purposelessness and despair shall not, after all, have the last word. God's promises to Israel and her expectations are not null, void, and empty. Something momentous is now happening. A birth will occur. A son will be born. Peace on earth is proclaimed.

If Advent means anything, it means that people have reason for expectation and hope. There is a word of encouragement and reassurance that vitally affects the fortunes of humankind and of each of us. The senseless and demonic slaughter of people, whether by pogrom or incineration, is not the last word. The television scenes of horrible hunger and starvation that give us indigestion over dinner are not the last word in a godless and indifferent world. Domestic strife, heartache, recrimination, alienation, and divorce are not the last word; neither are senility, incontinence, and the dissolution of a familiar human character and personality. The last word about us will not be the medical examiner's report.

The next-to-last word is that human history is not merely an interesting but dangerous merry-go-round. Something literally epoch-making has happened, is happening. We are going somewhere. The next-to-last word is that the virgin will conceive and bear a son. The last word is that the God manifest in that Son rules and will rule. The end is God. Therefore, life is good. We are blessed.

Do you believe that? The Gospel of Luke announces it to us. The annunciation to Mary is the announcement of good news. It is gospel, gospel truth. I cannot tell you whether or how to believe it. Nobody can.

Luke tells his story; we repeat it after him. If at times we hardly believe it or find it hard to believe, that is not surprising. Look around, and your suspicions that the world and the good old U.S.A. are not full of good tidings is quickly confirmed. Yet, there is just enough happening, or not happening, to suggest that this magnificent narrative of the advent of God's rule is not a fairy-tale, that is, a flight from reality into pleasant fantasy. People in this university community will respond in a tangible, if modest, way to the opportunity to help others who are starving. A man in Durham, North Carolina, who is himself poor, announces that he will give half his income to famine relief. Justice may not always be done in this world, but sometimes, surprisingly, it is done, and, in the words of Luke, the mighty are put down from their seats. Moreover, this happens just when and where ordinary folk simply fulfill their duties. Remarkably, despite the hatreds and strife that rend the fabric of humankind's unity, the world has been preserved until now. Of course there are no grounds for complacency, but there is ground for hope. Christian hope may be hoping against hope, but it is encouraged by tokens of God's graciousness and people's acceptance of it.

Thus the story still has power to excite and to awaken expectations: "You shall conceive and bear a son, and you shall give him the name Jesus. He will be great; he will bear the title Son of the Most High; the Lord God will give him the throne of his ancestor David, and he will be king over the house of Jacob forever; his reign shall never end." Yet Mary's question—"How can this be?"—is still very much our own, whether we think of Jesus' birth or the promise to mankind which it conveys. The angel's response refers Mary to God's power to make real the thing promised. Now, in Advent, Mary's question arouses hopeful expectancy and the anticipation of joy in our hearts. We too listen for the heaven-sent word of confirmation: "The Holy Spirit will come upon you, and the power of the Most High will overshadow you."

"Here am I," says Mary, "I am the Lord's servant; as you have spoken, so be it." So be it indeed!

Some matters relevant to a full exegesis of this text receive no emphasis in the sermon. For instance, that there were stories of miraculous births in the Old Testament, Judaism, and Greek mythology is at most acknowledged obliquely. Moreover, the importance of Israel and the Old Testament in Luke's literary and theological plan is only suggested. The possibility that Luke's birth narrative is a midrashic treatment of certain Old Testament texts is not considered. Nor is much direct attention given to the way the text and the entire birth narrative function in the development of Luke's theology. Yet Luke's central conception of salvation history underlies this text. The Old Testament language and motifs, as well as Gabriel's explicit announcement to Mary that she will conceive and bear a Davidic, messianic ruler, make this clear. The time of Israel leads up to and is fulfilled in the appearance of Jesus as the Messiah. After his ministry, death, resurrection, and ascension, there is the time of the church and its mission of spreading the gospel in the world. When this is accomplished, whether in many years or few, Jesus will return. Luke's viewpoint has come to dominate much Christian thinking about history.

Luke relates a miracle and literally takes us into another world, one defined by myth rather than science. The problem of demythologizing is not, however, named or treated systematically in the sermon. Nevertheless, a real effort is made to explore the theological validity and hermeneutical viability of Luke's intention in relating a miracle. This intention is, it seems to me, inescapable, as much as I myself tried to escape it in the initial stage of preparing this sermon. Just because the exegesis of the text convinced me of the importance of the miraculous dimension, it came to occupy a large place in the sermon.

We should again recall that ordinarily a sermon cannot deal with everything in a given text. If the preacher underlines the—or even a—principal motif or thrust of the text, he has done enough. The focus of a sermon upon the text, as well as the way in which one moves from text to sermon, naturally depends a great deal on the time and place of preaching. The preacher stands in a hermeneutical circle or ellipse, of which the human situation represented by a congregation at a given time and place is one pole and the text itself the other pole. In preaching, the burden of the text is not given by that human situation, but it is also not given apart from it. Thus the task of preaching is different from the task of exegesis, and from that of descriptive biblical theology, although both should inform preaching. But the degree to which they do may not always be entirely explicit in the sermon. Much more lies behind the sermon than appears in it. As a matter of principle, it is a good question whether the exegetically correct perspective on a text is best conveyed in the sermon by the recitation of exegetical procedures or results. When that happens, the sermon may lose its proper genre and become a lecture. And, it may be asked, who then becomes the authority for what is said, the Spirit and the Word or the letter, of which the exegetical scholar is master? There is always a danger it may be the latter.

It is nevertheless a fair question whether now standard exegetical procedures were helpful in illuminating this particular text for preaching. As a matter of fact, they were. Historical criticism, form criticism, and redaction criticism all made a contribution.

Did it happen? The old question, posed from the perspective of an older if somewhat naive historical criticism, can receive no answer that is not already programmed into it. Virgins do not conceive while they are virgins. Everyone acknowledges that. But Luke implies that a miracle is to occur. In one form or another the fact question keeps coming up, and although in that form it is poorly put, the reasons for asking it may be significant. Luke clearly wishes to convey something of the unique and momentous nature of Jesus' birth, and his Annunciation story does that. An earlier stage of history-of-religions investigation may have seen in parallel stories of miraculous births a way of disposing of the Gospel infancy narratives as variations of a not uncommon ancient myth. Such stories of course proved nothing against the historicity of the miraculous birth of Jesus to those who on other grounds were convinced of it. Yet the adduction of this evidence was important in other respects. The parallels suggest why Luke would have thought the annunciation of a virgin birth a proper and fitting way to begin his narrative. The motifs of miraculous birth and divine initiative in conception are not unknown in the Old Testament (Isaac, Jeremiah), and its influence was probably of fundamental importance in the formation of the Lucan birth narrative. Moreover, alleged parallels from the broader Hellenistic world are not insignificant in this regard, although they often attribute a sexual function to the divine being which is remarkably absent from Luke's account.

Form criticism of a hypothetical oral or preliterary tradition is hard to apply to our text, and the search for written sources is not likely to lead to agreement among scholars. But as Dibelius has suggested, there probably was an earlier, presumably oral, tradition which Luke has taken up. The very different Matthean account of the "annunciation" to Joseph with its strange agreements (virginity of Mary, conception by the Holy Spirit, role of Gabriel), as well as numerous and significant differences, suggests the existence of a tradition of the early church. (Probably the structural parallels with the annunciation to Zechariah of John the Baptist's birth are, however, the work of Luke and not to be attributed to a similar oral form of tradition.)

Redaction criticism, or composition criticism, affords the most fruitful avenue into this text, as might be expected, particularly when one asks broadly about the intention of Luke as it is reflected in the way he employs this narrative. The pattern he developed, centering as it does around the doublets of the annunciation and births of John the Baptist and Jesus, obviously accentuates a sense of expectancy, promise, and fulfillment. Thus Luke's conception of the history of salvation emerges. What is adumbrated in the case of the Baptist is fulfilled in Jesus. Mary's wonder before the power of God, perhaps indigenous to a pre-Lucan form of the narrative, is preserved and enhanced by Luke. Although he does not wish thereby to impart some astonishing biological fact about Jesus' conception, he nevertheless quite clearly intends the reader to understand the epoch-making character of what is about to transpire in the history of God's dealing with his people. It happens within Israel and fulfills her prophecies and hopes, yet in such a way as to transcend or transform them. The redemption of Israel expected by Zechariah (Luke 1:68) is to be accomplished by Jesus (Luke 24:21; Acts 1:6), but not in ways that could have been anticipated—not until Israel herself is judged (2:34–35; Acts 28:23–28) and, in effect, redefined. When God sends Israel on a new course—or back on the right course—he does so through humble agents but with astounding effect. All this is fore-shadowed by the annunciation to Mary.

We can suggest how in this case exegesis has led from text to sermon. It is more difficult, however, to generalize and to derive general principles governing that movement. The work of exegesis is essential, but how it may pay off is not guaranteed in advance. Exegesis helps define and guide the quest for meaning and truth, but it does not exhaust or limit the scope or meaning of the text as it speaks and is heard through the preacher or reader. The text has its own power to speak. At best, exegesis frees it. From my childhood this Annunciation text has aroused in me a sense of wonder and awe, along with joyous expectations. Exegesis indeed confirms that these feelings are grounded in the text and in the author's intention. But exegesis does not produce this initial sense of what the text is about, where it leads. In my case, however, it did revive it.

PART THREE

Preaching from the Gospel of John: A Different but Related Task

7

THE CHARACTER OF THE
FOURTH GOSPEL

THE INTERPRETATION of the Fourth Gospel for preaching must also proceed on the basis of an exegetically sound perspective and method. The fundamental exegetical question—What did the ancient author intend to say to his readers?—if asked consistently and honestly, will in the case of John as well as the other Gospels prove a reliable guide and a guard against the hazards of historicism on the one hand and allegorical interpretation on the other. Both these hazards, although polar opposites, imperil the exegesis of the Fourth Gospel in particular.

On the one hand, John's portrayal of Jesus and especially John's presentations of Jesus' words and discourses are often expounded from the pulpit as if they were verbatim historical reports. Such an interpretation, if advanced in all innocence, is understandable and scarcely reprehensible, and it is not entirely untrue to the intention and purpose of the evangelist, who wishes to anchor his presentation of the Christian preaching about Jesus in the preaching and deeds of Jesus. Yet the modern exegete and preacher, aware of the great disparity between the synoptic and Johannine portrayals of Jesus, can scarcely regard the Johannine as historical in view of the character of its divergences from the other three. Not only the three synoptic Gospels but also the strands of tradition represented in these Gospels (Mark and the hypothetical sources of Matthew and Luke: Q, M, and L), as well as those found in the Didache, the letters of Ignatius, and even the Gospel of Thomas, present a picture of Jesus that is substantially different from the Johannine. The fact that the Johannine Jesus proclaims himself, his messianic dignity and sonship, while as a rule in the other witnesses he does not, also raises serious questions about the historicity of John's representation. One may possibly plead that John supplements the other Gospels or traditions and provides another perspective on Jesus. Although this is in some sense true, it is not a consideration which necessarily supports the historicity of the Johannine view alongside the others. That the distinctive and characteristic traits of the Johannine portrayal of Jesus should be regarded as having the same, or greater, historical value is scarcely credible. For had Jesus actually spoken in the terms he employs in the Fourth Gospel, it is impossible to understand why the other Gospels and traditions should so little reflect this fact, inasmuch as the faith they too affirm is enunciated by the Johannine Jesus.

At the opposite end of the exegetical spectrum is the temptation to treat the Gospel as a series of symbols or an allegory. That is understandable in view of the character of the Gospel and the negative historical judgments rendered on it in the late nineteenth and early twentieth centuries. Yet such treatments of the Gospel were not unheard of in the precritical period. Indeed, the earliest known commentary on the Gospel, that of the Valentinian Gnostic Heracleon, was apparently of this sort. Moreover, the obvious theological emphasis of the Fourth Gospel seems to warrant discounting or ignoring any historical question or dimension.

Nevertheless, the historical question presses itself upon us, if not in the old form of whether the Fourth Gospel is an accurate eyewitness report of what Jesus said and did. As has been repeatedly observed, the evangelist is very much concerned about the historical question in both a broader and a narrower sense: broader in that according to his definition the history of Jesus does not stop on the date of his crucifixion but continues into the period of the early church; narrower in that he is principally interested only in the Christian theological significance of Jesus' historical ministry. Thus John portrays Jesus in controversy with those who reject the gospel message that he is the Son of God, while comforting, reassuring, and supporting those who have come to believe that message and thus are his disciples, his own. Jesus' ministry extends into the church's history as a prolongation of the struggle which began in his historical career. The issues have, however, narrowed or concentrated upon the decisive questions of who he is and what his appearance signifies. That is already an important question for Mark, for the tradition before him, and probably also for the contemporaries and disciples of the historical Jesus. But by John's time, in his community and in the history of that community's struggle with its Jewish and other rivals, the question of Jesus' identity has been narrowed down and cast in specifically Christian terms. This process of definition and refinement doubtless reflects both developments within the community and pressures and questions from outside. Thus the present Gospel embodies and sets before the reader the history of the preaching, experience, theological questions, and conflicts of what we may now call the Johannine Christian community. An accurate understanding and interpretation of the Fourth Gospel is hardly attainable without an adequate grasp of this history, although an exact and certain reconstruction of it probably lies forever beyond our grasp. The evangelist, however, holds the deep conviction that his presentation of Jesus is profoundly historical, in the sense that it accurately states the theological truth of who he was and continues to be.

So the question of history and the Fourth Gospel, while a complex one which admits of no simple answer, is not only allowable on the terms posed by the Gospel but is demanded and pressed upon us by it. Nevertheless, the historical question really merges into the theological one, for it ultimately becomes the question of whether the history of Jesus, known to us from other traditions (which may be found outside John and also isolated within that Gospel), will in any sense bear the interpretation John puts upon it. The evangelist and his school would not only answer affirmatively but would insist that precisely this interpretation is demanded by history and the tradition when rightly understood.

We are then in the Fourth Gospel confronted with an interpretation, by intention an interpretation of history, not an interpretation that ignores or willingly departs from history. If on the one side it is an interpretation—that is, not a chronicle of facts, not history or biography in any ordinary sense of those terms—then on the other it is an account, or an accounting, which intends to make the best sense of history that has become the object of controversy and division. It is a commentary on that history's origin in the light of subsequent reflection and controversy.

Thus in interpreting the Fourth Gospel we interpret an interpretation. This is true also in the case of the synoptic Gospels. The difference is simply this: In the synoptics the elements of tradition—many of which are primitive, not yet cast in distinctly Christian terms, often harking back to and representing the historical Jesus *as he actually was*—clearly obtrude. But in John the process of interpretation has gone much further, or deeper, so that the tradition of Jesus, where it is recognizable as such, has become permeated with the Johannine Christian interpretation of him. This is primarily true of the words and discourses of Jesus, but it is also to some extent true of the narratives, especially the signs, which are recounted in such a way as to underscore the initiative and role of Jesus. The key to an adequate and intellectually or theologically responsible interpretation of John is a recognition of the interpretative character of the narration, which avoids both the Scylla of an impossible historicism bound to yield negative results and the Charybdis of an allegorical symbolic or even theological interpretation which simply excludes any consideration of history.

Both to illustrate the character of the Fourth Gospel and to provide the basis for some concrete and specific guidelines and commentary which may prove helpful in preaching, we shall examine closely John 16, a section of the so-called farewell discourses of Jesus. Perhaps this part of John more than any other manifests its distinctiveness over against the synoptic Gospels.

8

THE EXEGESIS OF THE FOURTH GOSPEL: JESUS' FAREWELL (John 16)

THE GOSPEL of John is thoroughly Christian, and in a sense that even the synoptic Gospels are not. That is, in John, Jesus utters the Christian confession or credo and places himself, his person and work, at the center of his teaching. John 16 and the farewell discourses (John 14–16) generally are, however, even more distinctively Christian than the rest of the Gospel in that here Jesus in speaking to his disciples anticipates their situation after he has departed from them. Thus in effect he speaks to the postresurrection church. The problems addressed are uniquely and explicitly Christian. By the device of describing in advance the future situation, Jesus addresses the present existence of Johannine Christians, and so the Christian moment or dimension of the Fourth Gospel emerges in complete clarity.

It is difficult to break up John 15–16 even for purposes of analysis, since the several various themes and emphases interlock. By looking closely at John 16, however, we may identify the principal points made by Jesus in the farewell discourses.

In John 16:1–4 Jesus concludes his discussion of the hatred of the world for the disciples which began in 15:18 (cf. also the reprise in 17:14). The effects of this hatred are now specified (16:2): The disciples will be put out of synagogues (cf. 9:22; 12:42) and even killed. The threat of expulsion from the synagogues probably envisions an actual situation in which Jews who confessed Jesus as the Christ were excluded from the fellowship of the Jewish community. This was obviously an important if not epoch-making turning point in the history of the Johannine Christian community. Followers of Jesus in this and other Christian communities did not originally intend that by confessing Jesus to be the Christ (or Messiah) of Jewish expectation they should cease to be Jews. Jesus himself never thought of giving up Judaism to found a new religion. Paul, when he wants to speak of the person who is obedient to God, writes: "He is a Jew who is one inwardly. . . . His praise is not from men but from God" (Rom. 2:29). Apparently the Johannine community has within recent memory felt the trauma of expulsion from the house of Israel. What is anticipated as a fearful consequence in John 9:22 and 12:42 is firmly predicted in 16:2, which reflects the situation of the Christian circles which produced the Gospel. This state of affairs probably points to a stage in Jewish-Christian relations after the Roman War (A.D. 66–70) and during the retrenchment of Judaism which followed, when Christians were threatened with expulsion from the Jewish community because they confessed Jesus to be the Messiah. Certainly it does not reflect the situation of Jesus' own time.

Whether or not Jewish Christians were also executed or subject to fear of execution by their fellow Jews, as John 16:2 may be taken to imply, is an important question. That such a mortal threat did not lie outside the realm of possibility may also be inferred from John's descriptions of the deadly hostility of the Jews to Jesus. Such descriptions may in fact reflect a continuing mortal hatred toward Jesus' emissaries. The Jewish character of the opposition seems to be implicit in the belief of those who kill Christians that they are "offering service to God." (The Greek term rendered "service," *latreia,* is a common one for worship.) On the other hand, Christians were widely considered impious or atheists by their pagan contemporaries, and the statement in question may simply refer—admittedly in Jewish or Christian terms— to the religious reasons for persecuting Christians. It is difficult to say on the basis of our rather fragmentary and allusive evidence whether Jews per se were in fact subjecting Johannine Christians to mortal threat. Yet in view of the harshly polemical tone displayed on both sides in the Gospel debates between Jesus and the Jews, that possibility must be taken seriously.[1]

In any event, a growing hostility between Jews and Christians is reflected at this and other points in the Gospel. Undoubtedly hostility and conflict played a significant role in the development of the Christian consciousness which produced the Fourth Gospel. The memory of the separation from the synagogue is still vivid in the Johannine community. Otherwise the strong sense of the demarcation of the community from the world, and particularly from the Jews, would be difficult to understand. A sectarian self-consciousness is strongly reflected in the dualism of the Johannine writings and in the awareness that, unlike the synagogue and the world, the Christians believe in and belong to Jesus.[2]

Yet the opponents, the outsiders, are not only or at least not necessarily Jews. In John 16:3 Jesus says that the murderous opposition he has just described springs from not knowing the Father or himself (obviously an ignorance of his true origin, goal, and nature). This description would, on Johannine terms, apply to unbelievers and opponents other than Jews. Whether or not such heathen rejection of the gospel and its representatives is envisioned is debatable, but the description is principally appropriate. Moreover, the opposition is initially described as the *world's* hatred (John 15:18–19). Jewish rejection or persecution of Jesus and his followers is apparently the archetype of the world's opposition; in fact, in surrendering itself to Caesar, Judaism becomes the world (John 19:15). But the world's opposition is not limited to Judaism, although the Jews have become representative of the world. It is thus accurate to say that in John the Jews represent the world, but one should not discount the role the synagogue and certain Jews have actually played in the evolution of Johannine theology and styles of speech. A genuine church-synagogue dialogue and conflict underlies the Fourth Gospel.

Apparently John 16:1 and 16:4 serve to frame the important word of 16:2–3 and to call attention to the setting and purpose for which it is intended. Jesus speaks of things which the church will remember and appreciate only in the light of its subsequent, postresurrection history (cf. John 2:17, 22; 7:39; 12:16). Indirectly, Christians are admonished to take note of Jesus' predictions (John 16:4). The motif of the importance of the disciples' later recollection and interpretation of events and Jesus' word is an important one in the Gospel, particularly in the farewell discourses, as an examination of the rest of this chapter will confirm.

In John 16:4b one can discern a recognition and understanding of the fact that the things Jesus is portrayed as saying on the eve of his departure were not part of his message during his public ministry. It was not necessary for Jesus to explain some things to his followers while he himself was still with them. Now, however, he leaves them to go to the Father. The question Jesus says none of his disciples is asking him (John 16:5) has in effect been asked in 14:5. Perhaps this seeming anomaly can be explained by the fact that two independent farewell discourses (John 14; John 15–16) have been conjoined in the final redaction of the Gospel. Alternatively, the anomaly may function as a means of returning to the theme of John 14. Jesus departs from his disciples, and his departure is the cause of perplexity and even sorrow. The discourses are intended to explain his departure and to allay such feelings of despair.

What then is the meaning of Jesus' departure? First of all, which departure is referred to? The departure and absence of Jesus after his death, that is, between his death and resurrection appearances, or after his resurrection, that is, the ascension? Verse 7 seems to indicate that the latter is primarily in view, for only after the resurrection does the Spirit come (John 20:22; cf. 7:39). Traditionally in early Christian thought the Spirit appears in the time between the resurrection and the Parousia. The word *Counselor* in the Revised Standard Version translates the Greek *parakletos*.[3] He is the Spirit of truth (John 15:26; 16:13) or the Holy Spirit (14:26). The exact meaning of this term in John, or why John uses this particular term of the Holy Spirit in the discourses, has never been satisfactorily determined. In the King James Version it was inadequately translated "Comforter." In 1 John 2:1 the term is used of Jesus, and in the Revised Standard Version it is translated "advocate," which corresponds to its etymological and generally accepted meaning. *The New English Bible* adopts this translation in the Gospel as well. It is at least partially justified by the fact that at the first mention of the Paraclete (John 14:16) he is called "another paraclete," an expression that seems to take up the understanding of Jesus as Paraclete (advocate) found in 1 John 2:1. To some extent the translation "advocate" suits the function of Jesus in the Fourth Gospel, especially in the farewell discourses. Jesus is the advocate of his disciples before the Father (cf. John 17). Yet it remains a question whether this term adequately covers every function as it is set forth there.

Undoubtedly because of the immediately preceding discussion of the world's hatred, the relation of the Paraclete to the world comes under consideration (John 16:8–11). In effect his work is to expose and condemn the error and sinfulness of the world in rejecting Jesus. But by and large the interest in the work of the Paraclete vis-à-vis the world is secondary. In the main John is concerned with the way the Paraclete functions in the church, that is, in relation to the disciples. To this theme, so characteristic of the farewell discourses, Jesus turns again in John 16:12–15.

The most startling aspect of what is now said about the Spirit of truth concerns his revelatory function. It appears that the Spirit of truth is to give the disciples additional revelations (John 16:12–13). The notion of the Spirit's bringing additional revelations, or of the risen, exalted Jesus' giving additional revelations through the Spirit, was not uncommon in early Christianity as Revelation 1–3 clearly shows. Moreover, even Paul has words of the Lord Jesus that are apparently given him through direct revelation or inspiration rather than by tradition (2 Cor. 12:8–9). The potential danger of such claims to unique, personal revelations is not hard to see. Therefore, "spirits" must be tested to see whether they are from God (1 John 4:1; cf. 1 Thess. 5:21). Doubtless the author(s) of the Gospel of John and the Johannine letters lived in a Christian community, or communities, in which Spirit-inspired utterances were not uncommon. The potential danger of such utterances was real, but they were not to be simply suppressed or rejected. There were criteria by which the validity of revelations or "spirits" could be judged (1 John 4:1–3). In the farewell discourses, Jesus himself makes clear that the Spirit does not reveal any and every sort of thing. That he does not speak on his own authority (John 16:13) means that what he has the right to say and reveal is subject to the authority of Jesus. He utters what he hears—from Jesus—and "declares the things that are to come." That is, the Spirit of prophecy speaks only on Jesus' authority even while he interprets the unfolding future to the community of Jesus' followers.[4] At this point there seem to be striking parallels between the utterances of Jesus in the farewell discourses and the way the Lord, the Spirit, and the prophet relate to each other and function in the Book of Revelation (esp. chaps. 1–3). While it is plain that the Spirit's role is to expound to the community the revelation given in Jesus, it is not so obvious how that revelation in Jesus is understood and what this unfolding of that revelation really amounts to.

Although John makes clear that the Spirit speaks only on Jesus' authority, taking what is Jesus' and declaring it to the disciples (or the church), it remains a question how "what is mine" (that is, Jesus') is understood in relation to the historical Jesus and the tradition about him. Quite possibly the key is found in John 16:15, "All that the Father has is mine." Revelations of the Spirit which are authentically God-given are also from Jesus. Thus all true Spirit-inspired revelation glorifies Jesus and is the declaration of his truth. To say this, however, is not helpful in solving the problem of distinguishing authentic from inauthentic spirits or revelations. But perhaps just because the problem is left unresolved in the Fourth Gospel it must be dealt with in 1 John.

When one reviews all the Paraclete sayings (John 14:15–17, 25–26; 15:26–27; 16:12–15) and related passages, however, it is evident that the evangelist does not wish to say simply that every true revelation of God is a revelation of Jesus without in any way specifying what Jesus may or may not be or represent. The Spirit bears witness to Jesus (John 15:26), who is clearly understood to be a historical figure out of the past. He brings to *remembrance* all Jesus has said to his disciples (John 14:26). Earlier the importance of the disciples' retrospectively recalling and understanding what Jesus has said to them is underlined (John 2:17, 22; 12:16). John does not wish to say that every revelation from God is a revelation of Jesus without indicating what may be a revelation of God. It is in fact Jesus who defines a revelation from God. He is God's revelation *(logos)*, and Jesus is clearly understood to be a concrete historical figure who among other things reveals that God is love (John 3:16), loves his own (13:1), and commands that they love one another (13:34–35). He is not anything anybody wants to make him. Nevertheless, the question remains as to how the continuing revelation of God in Jesus relates to the historical Jesus in the author's own understanding. That problem is plainly evident in the very considerable difference between John and the synoptics, in which the tradition of Jesus, particularly Jesus' words, has not to any comparable degree been suffused with Christian theological and polemical interests, as well as Christian piety and spirituality.

It is by no means unreasonable to surmise that the specific function of the Spirit-Paraclete as described in the Fourth Gospel is actually represented in the figure and words of the Johannine Jesus. Not only the Christian-Jewish polemic of the first-century community and the accompanying Christian confession of Jesus comes to expression in John. Also reflected in this Gospel are inspired utterances of those empowered by the Spirit to speak in his name and in the first person.[5] That is, the words of Jesus, so different from the synoptic tradition, may be based upon Spirit-inspired prophetic utterance. If so, this would account both for their distinctiveness and for their authoritative ring.

In John 16:16–24 we find a long discussion of the saying of Jesus about "a little while" (vv. 16 and 19). This saying occurs also in another form in John 14:19; related sayings appear in 7:33–34, 8:21, 12:35, and 13:33. At the root of such passages there was doubtless a traditional word of Jesus, well-known in Johannine circles. The sayings in John 7:33–34, 8:21, and 12:35 all speak of or allude to the departure of Jesus and are addressed to the Jews or to the public; the same is true of John 13:33, which although addressed to the disciples refers to what Jesus has said previously to the Jews. The problem of the authenticity of this saying, or some form of it, need not concern us. Our question has to do with its meaning at this point in the Gospel. As the questioning of the disciples develops (John 16:17–18) and Jesus renders a rather enigmatic answer (vv. 19ff.), one of two possible interpretations of the text must be chosen. Is Jesus talking about his departure in death and return in the resurrection, or is he talking about his departure at the Ascension and his return at the end of history? Presumably the former. The Parousia interpretation seems already excluded by the statement of Judas in John 14:22 and Jesus' answer, which confirms its correctness. Moreover, the disciples' sorrow, contrasted with the world's rejoicing (v. 20), is apparently a reference to divergent reactions to the crucifixion of Jesus. The apparent allusion to prayer in Jesus' name (vv. 23, 26–27) has in view the postresurrection time of the church rather than the Parousia. The references to seeing Jesus again (John 16:16, 19) then apply to his resurrection appearances.

Nevertheless, the Parousia of Jesus is also indirectly in view, for one purpose of the farewell discourses is to assure the disciples that they will not be left alone in the world (John 14:18). This purpose hovers in the background of our text. Jesus appears to his disciples after his death, but these appearances terminate. John knows this from common Christian tradition. When the appearances end, Christians are not left to face the world alone; Jesus continues to be with them through the Spirit, even though he does not appear to them. They can now pray to the Father in Jesus' name and he will hear (16:23, 26–27). Thus Jesus' departure to the Father from whom he came (16:28; cf. 17:8; 5:19) is

grounds for his disciples' rejoicing. Because he goes away, the Counselor or Paraclete (16:7), who represents an extension and continuation
of the revelation of God in Jesus, comes.

At first glance the promise of John 16:25 may seem more naturally to
refer to the return of Jesus, that is, to his Parousia. Yet as we have
already noted, the discussion of the disciples' praying "in that day"
indicates that the time of the church is in view. The speaking in figures to
which Jesus alludes (v. 25) refers to the discussion which has immediately preceded (vv. 16–24); the plain speaking which he promises
actually occurs in verse 28. The response of the disciples (vv. 29–30),
"Ah, now you are speaking plainly, not in any figure!..." confirms this.
The farewell discourses end with Jesus' speaking the truth plainly to his
disciples, and with their comprehending.

Just at that point, however, Jesus expresses a curious reservation
about their belief (John 16:31–32). How is this to be accounted for? In
part by tradition. The abandonment of Jesus by his disciples after his
arrest and arraignment is thoroughly fixed in the memory and traditions
of early Christianity (cf. Mark 14:27, 50). Although in Mark it is
embodied in an Old Testament quotation (Zech. 13:7), in all probability it has a historical basis, for Christians would not likely have con-
trived a story so unflattering to the disciples. Nevertheless, this seems a
strange place for John to introduce the tradition. Jesus has just spoken
plainly to the disciples and they have professed to understand him. Then
quite suddenly and for no apparent reason Jesus abruptly calls their
understanding into question.

The solution to this puzzle is probably to be found in the peculiar
perspective of the Fourth Gospel. Throughout the Gospel, Jesus himself
speaks in Christian, confessional terms with a full knowledge of what is
about to transpire. In the farewell discourses this knowledge applies
particularly to the Johannine Christian church. But the disciples, although they recognize Jesus for who he is when they first meet him
(John 1) and are said to believe in him after his first public act (2:11),
maintain and in the farewell discourses still manifest an ignorance
about the most important matters (14:5ff.). In this respect the Johannine portrayal of the disciples before the crucifixion and resurrection is
not unlike the Marcan portrayal.[6] Thus even here Jesus points to and
reflects upon the significant, residual admixture of unbelief that colors
and taints the disciples' profession of their faith in him. While he speaks

with full Christian knowledge, that is, knowledge that reflects the historical and doctrinal data on which Christian faith is built, they lack such knowledge and are unable to digest it even when Jesus expounds it to them. Such knowledge, the author knows, is really inappropriate to them until they have witnessed Jesus' crucifixion and experienced the reality of his resurrection (cf. esp. John 20:26–29).

Jesus concludes the discourse by telling his disciples that he has spoken as he has so that they may have peace (John 16:33; cf. the peace Jesus bestows in 14:27). But his words are not so much an explanation they can immediately assimilate as a heritage upon which they shall draw. His final statement ("In the world you have tribulation; but be of good cheer, I have overcome the world") is a word of realism and hope. Troubles are as real as the world is, but the disciples are not to be dismayed. They shall remain in the world (John 17:15) but will not be overcome by it; for Jesus, in apparently succumbing to the world's judgment of him, has really judged (12:31–32; cf. 3:17–19; 16:8–11) and overcome the world.

A singular feature of the Fourth Gospel, which has already been observed in the exegetical discussion, makes the task of preaching from it somewhat different from the task of preaching from the synoptics. We have emphasized that the material, the tradition, of the synoptics had its setting in life in the preaching, worship, and other activities of primitive Christianity. Stories and sayings of Jesus are, broadly speaking, put in the service of preaching. Indeed, in compositions such as the Sermon on the Mount, sayings of Jesus became the material out of which sermon-like compositions are constructed. (The Sermon on the Mount is nowhere called that in Matthew or anywhere else in the New Testament, but the traditional name for it is entirely apt.) Quite possibly, miracle stories took on symbolic meaning in the preaching of the early church. In any event, they sometimes have such significance in the synoptics. Thus the miracles of restoration of sight to the blind that open and close the central complex of Mark (chapters 8–10) clearly have a symbolic meaning. They symbolize the movement from ignorance—lack of perception about the nature of Jesus' messiahship and of discipleship—to perception and understanding, which is the theme of that section.

John, however, goes further in developing what we may call the symbolic and sermonic function of the Jesus tradition. This difference between John and the synoptics may be graphically stated in some such fashion as this: Whereas the synoptics incorporate stories and sayings of Jesus as texts or illustrations of sermons, or for sermons, John contains explicitly Christian sermons. John 16 is in effect if not a sermon of Jesus a running dialogue between Jesus and his disciples. This dialogue nevertheless has a sermonic function, for it brings to expression certain important aspects of the relationship of the departed and exalted Jesus, and his Spirit, to his disciples who constitute his church on earth. As we have seen, Jesus tells his disciples things they cannot really know or appreciate until after resurrection faith has emerged among them. Before he goes he tells the disciples things they can understand only after he has departed.

Thus John gives to the preacher who follows him more explicit guidance for preaching than one expects or finds in the synoptics. In speaking to the disciples, the Jesus of John speaks directly to the postresurrection church. Ironically, those disciples do not understand Jesus, even in the Johannine narrative, as well as the Christian reader can. John thus sets Christian preachers on the way they should want to go. It is conceivable that a Jewish sermon or a general religious discourse could be preached from at least some synoptic texts, taken in isolation. A Johannine text, however, scarcely allows for anything other than an explicitly Christian (in a theological sense) sermon. Of course, general sermons in praise of truth have doubtless been preached on such a text as John 8:32: "You will know the truth, and the truth will make you free." Yet such a sermon is possible only if the verse is removed from its highly christological (indeed, polemical) context and if that context is completely ignored by the preacher.

Context is crucially important in preaching from John. Moreover, the Johannine context has distinctive traits. In the first place, as is well illustrated by John 16, the literary context of any specific text or pericope is likely to be larger in John than in the synoptics. Moreover, the context of material is closely knit. A saying, parable, or story in the synoptics, for example, Mark 12:13–17, may be relatively independent of its context. One must say "relatively" because Mark obviously put a controversy story such as 12:13–17, or the complex to which it belongs, where he did for a purpose. But it does not depend principally or entirely upon its context in order to be understood, although its context should be considered in interpreting it. John, however, is different. Once again John 16 will serve to illustrate the point. There is no part of that entire complex that can for a moment stand by itself in the sense that it can have its proper meaning outside its context in John 16, or indeed in the farewell discourses. The famous saying of John 16:33—"In the world you have tribulation; but be of good cheer, I have overcome the world"—affords a good example of this fact. It is not a general moral or spiritual maxim but the final utterance of the earthly Jesus to his community, and one that they cannot yet understand!

Something more must also be said about the *total* context of the Gospel of John. Earlier it was suggested that much of the Gospel (John 16:1–4 in particular, as well as John 9) mirrors the conflict between Judaism and Christianity, which was the historical matrix that gave birth to the Fourth Gospel. There is much evidence to indicate that this is the case. Yet while the germinal importance of the controversy is plain, the evidence which points so clearly to it has been set by the evangelist within a broader scope of Christian theological interest. This broader scope is typified by the literary structure of the Gospel. In it the public ministry of Jesus is framed at the beginning by the prologue and at the end by the farewell discourses, of which we have examined a representative portion. The prologue centers around the theme of the cosmic significance of Jesus Christ. The farewell discourses deal, as we have observed, with pressing Christian theological issues such as eschatology, that is, the coming again of Jesus. Moreover, at the end of the original form of the Gospel (without John 21, which is apparently a later addition), in the dialogue between Jesus and "doubting Thomas," the distinctly Christian issue of seeing and believing as it relates to the risen Jesus emerges. Therefore, as far as preaching from John is concerned, there is reason enough for not taking the synagogue controversy per se as the context which endows the entire Gospel with its meaning and purpose. In practical terms, this means that, in preaching from John 16:1–4 or John 9, the Jewish-Christian controversy, which could easily be paralleled in the present day, need not be regarded as the sole or necessarily the primary point of the text, even of the text viewed as a historical document. Who are the Jewish opponents of Jesus, the unbelievers? At one stage they were certainly real Jews, especially leaders of the Pharisees who emphatically rejected the claims made for Jesus and probably drove his followers out of synagogues. The evangelist was, perhaps personally, still in touch with that stage. But he had himself already gone beyond it in the sense that the issue of belief and unbelief as he now understood it was no longer simply an issue dividing Christians, or followers of Jesus, from their fellow Jews. It divided the followers of Jesus from all those who had heard or might hear the gospel and not believe it. Furthermore, it divided the cosmos between light and darkness, the forces above and those beneath. Here the famous Johannine dualism comes into play.

So we arrive again at an earlier point, which in this connection also is valid: John is a distinctly and distinctively Christian rendition of the gospel genre. To preach from that Gospel is to preach from an explicitly Christian text. Thus John ought to be, and is, easily amenable to Christian preaching. At the same time, one must also say that if the synoptic Gospels resist being treated as historical or biographical documents, John resists such treatment all the more.

9

PROBLEMS AND PERSPECTIVES
IN PREACHING FROM
JOHN AND THE SYNOPTICS

HAVING EXAMINED John 16 closely, we may now ask again about problems and perspectives in preaching from John, and from the Gospels generally. Needless to say, the kind of attention we have given this text should precede and undergird preaching from any Gospel text. But since preaching is not the same as exegesis, a sermon may not yet be in hand even when one has done the necessary exegesis. Moreover, when a text has been thoroughly studied, certain questions, which can still be classified as exegetical, may remain.

One of these questions is how any specific text is related to other New Testament texts. Such a question can lead into the realm of systematic, or even practical, theology, but it may also be dealt with exegetically or historically. How does the situation which produced this text (or an entire Gospel) relate chronologically, geographically, or theologically to the situation that produced other New Testament texts? Are the texts themselves related? Such a determination may be significant for interpretation. As far as preaching from the Gospels is concerned, the question of their relationship can be of paramount importance. For example, does one interpret a Gospel (namely, Matthew, Luke, or John) on the assumption that the author knew one or more of the others?

As a general rule, when preaching from the synoptic Gospels it is advisable to concentrate primarily upon a pericope or a text as it appears in some one of them. The task of trying to reconstruct an original saying or scene on the basis of two or more renditions is one best left to the specialist. While the preacher may be, and should be, prepared for such an undertaking, it is ordinarily too complex for a single sermon. It is of course perfectly legitimate and sometimes even helpful to use parallel texts to illumine one another. On the assumption that Matthew knew Mark, the Marcan version of the parable of the sower was used to help interpret the Matthean version, on which the sermon was based. (Nevertheless, one should remember that Matthew did not expect the reader to have Mark before him as well.) The Matthean infancy narrative was also used to illumine the Lucan narrative. What would not have been legitimate, at least as historical exegesis, would have been to construct a composite narrative from parts of Matthew and Luke. In all probability Luke did not know Mattthew, and vice versa. There are many elements of the two stories that do not fit together, although there are also other congruent elements. To attempt to put them together, as happens in nativity scenes and plays, is to indulge in a rough-and-ready harmonization that fails to do justice to these distinct and different narratives. It is to make the historicist prejudgment about the nature and purpose of the narratives with which we are dealing. As a general rule, preaching from single pericopes or texts presents fewer pitfalls than the practice of combining texts from different Gospels, for whatever reasons and on whatever basis.

This rule applies also to the Fourth Gospel and the synoptics. John should not be harmonized with the synoptics. As John 16 clearly shows, the Fourth Gospel is of a different order. Yet John can scarcely be interpreted as if the others did not exist. We are faced with a not altogether simple problem. A generation or two ago, as throughout most of Christian history, one could take it for granted that John knew the synoptic Gospels, or at least Mark, and wrote with them in view, whether to supplement or interpret them. In light of more recent research and discussion of the question of their relationship, this can no longer be assumed. While it is not inconceivable that John wrote with knowledge of the synoptic Gospels, it is scarcely possible to demonstrate that he did. Moreover, the question of why, if John knew the synoptics, he wrote a Gospel which is both so different in style and context and yet in certain respects so similar (especially, but not only in the passion narratives), is at best still unanswered. Whether it can be answered is at this point in the history of scholarship and interpretation at least doubtful.

Some of the implications of this situation for the task of preaching should now become clear. If one could assume that John knew the other

Gospels and wrote with them constantly in view, the Fourth Gospel would then be interpreted against the background of the synoptics, whether positively or negatively. Although until recently most commentators have assumed that John not only knew the synoptics but also accepted them as valid, there is no longer unanimity on this point. Indeed, it has been seriously argued that John wrote in light of what he regarded as the deficiencies of the other Gospels and in order to correct or displace them. In any event, the assumption that John knew the synoptics and wrote with them in mind, if adhered to rigorously, will greatly influence the interpretation of the Fourth Gospel. John will be viewed as supplementing, interpreting, or even correcting the synoptic presentation, and that assumption will affect the exegesis of specific texts.

What if it is not taken for granted that John knew the synoptics? Most of what is found in the synoptics is unaccountably missing in John, and vice versa. If one thinks it unlikely that John knew the other Gospels, or at least that his Gospel was influenced or determined by them, one can nevertheless not ignore them in exegeting the Fourth Gospel. Even if John did not derive his material from any of the synoptics, he obviously knew some oral or written traditions similar to those employed by the synoptists. That much, at least, is certain. This problem did not arise directly when we examined John 16, for there we found a discourse of Jesus that has no direct parallel in the synoptics. In its distinct language and theology, as well as in the way it reflects its historical setting, that text is typically Johannine. But when, for example, we read John's account of the feeding of the five thousand or the cleansing of the temple, we shall likely conclude he is describing the same event that is found in the synoptics. The cleansing affords us an interesting and thorny example of the problem the relationship of John and the synoptics poses for the interpreter, particularly if one gives priority to the historical question.

John places the cleansing near the beginning of his Gospel (chapter 2), while in all the synoptics it is found in the passion narrative. If we believe that John knew the synoptics, we must decide whether the fourth evangelist relates another, similar incident, which is improbable, or corrects or at least changes the synoptics by moving the incident forward in his narrative. If exegetes pursue the historical question on the assumption that it is the same incident, they must next decide which—John or the synoptics—actually has it in the historically correct position. Historical probability would then seem to be on the side of this event's having occurred late, shortly before Jesus' arrest, rather than at the beginning of his ministry. The accusation that Jesus was a threat to the temple in the Marcan version of the trial before the Sanhedrin falls into place soon after the cleansing. Such an action provides a motivation for the hostility that leads to Jesus' death, although it is not expressly cited in the trials. Granting the correctness of the synoptic version, it is perhaps easier to conceive of John's moving forward an incident he knew only by tradition as associated with the passion than to conceive of his moving an incident whose position was already fixed in another narrative account of Jesus' ministry, that is, in another Gospel. But if John did not know our synoptic Gospels, it is even conceivable that his traditional account of the cleansing was not specifically associated with the passion.

With C. H. Dodd, Raymond E. Brown, and others, I am inclined to think that the fourth evangelist did not know the synoptics; certainly he was not much influenced by them in composing his own work. If in the exegesis of this text for preaching we proceed on that assumption, which seems to me to be the more prudent course, we are not brought so abruptly face-to-face with the question of a seeming historical contradiction. Thus our exegesis will not be in danger of being deflected onto a historicist sidetrack. We may then pursue, as one should in any event, the question of the meaning of the temple cleansing within the Gospel according to John. Exegesis with that question in view will certainly prove to be more productive for preaching than the pursuit of the historical question. (Yet the interpreter may still find reason to think that John deliberately moved forward an incident he knew was associated with Jesus' passion.)

There is another sense in which the interpretation of the Fourth Gospel for preaching cannot ignore the synoptics. Obviously, all four Gospels belong together in the Christian canon of Scripture, and all purport to be about the same Jesus. The preacher cannot and should not keep the Gospels forever in watertight compartments separate from each other. Not even the Fourth Gospel can be segregated from the other three. The question then arises, How should they be related to one another in preaching? For the reasons already suggested, one should not indiscriminately or eclectically paint a picture of Jesus by plucking details first from the synoptics and then from John. It is in part a question of intellectual integrity. Sayings and scenes from John are often of a sort different from those in the synoptics. One cannot put them on the same level with regard either to historical character or to literary and traditional form. More important, there are theological and exegetical reasons which speak against running any of the Gospels together in this way.

If interpreters think that the burden of Scripture—or the word of God or its revelatory aspect—inheres not only in events or sayings or historical details but also in the genre of the literary documents that compose the New Testament, they will hesitate to rend the fabric of those documents carelessly by picking one thread here and another there to weave them into another tapestry; rather, they will respect their integrity. Certainly one would not wish to maintain that revelation occurs only in the Gospels, or other New Testament documents, any more than that revelation occurs only in the historical events themselves. The original Christian revelation, or the originative events of Christianity, were doubtless real in themselves, but their reality is now accessible and meaningful to us only in the New Testament documents, particularly the Gospels. Exegesis should respect not only the events to which the documents point but also the documents themselves. The events as sources of the Christian revelation are no more independent of the Gospels that convey them to us than the Gospels as sources of the revelation are independent of the events. In other words, if the interpreter does not respect the Gospels, the gospel itself is in danger of being lost.

To illustrate and underscore this point we may refer once again to Zeffirelli's television film *Jesus of Nazareth*. Because neither the plot line nor the order of events of any of the canonical Gospels is followed, another way of making things hang together must be found. In particular, it becomes necessary to find or construct another set of circumstances and a motivation for Jesus' death. This is done, none too clearly, by suggesting a link with Jewish Zealots through Judas Iscariot. Jesus is not a Zealot, but Judas attempts to portray Jesus to the Zealots as the leader to whom they should look. Yet Jesus does not satisfy the Zealots. Barabbas, who turns out to be a Zealot leader, is perplexed and put off when Jesus encounters him at the temple and admonishes him, saying, "All that take the sword shall perish by the sword." Zerah, a fictional Sadducean leader and member of the Sanhedrin, finally decides that Jesus must die when, again at the temple, Jesus gives sight to a blind man (John 9) and immediately thereafter denounces the Pharisees (Matthew 23). Subsequently, Judas, disillusioned and confused, is persuaded to hand Jesus over to the Sanhedrin for its judgment on his claim to be the Messiah. As an explanation of the reasons for Jesus' execution, all this is scarcely more plausible historically, and certainly less satisfying theologically and artistically, than the simple synoptic "the Son of man must suffer" or the Johannine "the Son of man must be lifted up." A historical explanation, which, murky as it may be, tends to exclude the will and salvation of God in favor of human machinations only, transforms the story of Jesus from the story of salvation into an interesting historical tale, trimmed with vestiges of the miraculous. It is a secular *Novelle*, to use Dibelius's category.

It is interesting that a couple of other dramatic presentations of Jesus have encountered greater critical and, within a narrower spectrum, popular success. Pasolini's *The Gospel according to St. Matthew* enjoyed far more critical acclaim than have most cinematic efforts to present the Bible. Without at all detracting from that director's skill, it might be suggested that a part of the film's success resulted from the decision to produce the Gospel of Matthew rather than to assemble a potpourri from all the Gospels. By the same token, Alec McCowen's dramatic recitation of *St. Mark's Gospel* in King James English, a performance that lasts for two hours, has played to packed theaters and enthusiastic reviews on both sides of the Atlantic. Reviewers have not failed to notice that McCowen has succeeded in bringing to light the simple, even primitive, but nonetheless powerful, dramatic quality of Mark's Gospel. Neither Pasolini, a Communist, nor McCowen considered himself engaged in any sort of Christian or religious undertaking. Yet by following the lead of the New Testament Gospels rather than succumbing to misbegotten historicist temptations, each succeeded in creating a work of religious as well as artistic significance. Unwittingly, they confirm the view that the burden of biblical revelation is in the literature as well as the history, or in the nexus between them. If the medium is not the message, neither can the message be divorced from the medium.

The presentation of McCowen may enjoy an additional advantage. Like the Gospel itself it relies on the word rather than on a visual image.

Ꮟ Ꮺ Ꮻ Ꮻ Ᏸ

In all probability, the original Gospel of Mark, like other Gospels in the early church, had its primary impact through being read aloud in churches, not as an object of individual, private meditation and study. McCowen's dramatization, carried out with a minimum of props, stage effects, and other action, is primarily an oral and aural event. Thus McCowen's version of Mark in all likelihood recreates something of the early, original, or even the intended, effect of that Gospel. So although McCowen achieves certain effects, for example, humor, that may not clearly belong to the evangelist's intention, he, like the evangelist himself, communicates primarily through the power of the word.

To do justice to the full range of portrayals of Jesus in the Gospels, it is not necessary or helpful to mix them together. What is true for dramatic or cinematic art is true also for preaching. It suffices to preach regularly from each Gospel on its own terms. Thus the principle of the lectionary, which constrains the preacher and the congregation to attend individually to the several Gospels, as well as the full range of Scripture, is a valid one.

Returning to the question of John and the synoptics, there are in summary at least two ways in which preaching from the Fourth Gospel will be influenced by the others. In the first place, because of its relation to the synoptic Gospels or synoptic tradition, John cannot be interpreted in isolation from them. Nevertheless, because of their different character and because the extent and nature of the relationship between them remains uncertain, the interpreter should exercise caution in relating Johannine and synoptic texts, limiting himself to matters that are obvious. One cannot safely assume that wherever John differs from the synoptics he is making some point over against them; there are many differences that seem fortuitous, inconsequential, or inexplicable. Second, preaching from John will also be influenced or balanced by the fact that the Fourth Gospel stands alongside the synoptics in the New Testament. But the interests of that influence or balance can better be served by preaching from both separately than by mixing them together in exegesis and preaching. John as a literary, theological document provides adequate clues for its own interpretation, but a Christian congregation which heard only preaching from John would likely receive a distorted picture of Christ. By the same token, a congregation which heard only preaching from the synoptics would receive an incomplete picture of him.

CONCLUSION

THIS BOOK is itself intended to be a kind of summation of the bearing of modern gospel criticism upon the task of interpreting the Gospels for preaching. So to sum up in any detail would be redundant and pointless. But certain essential and recurrent points, already explicitly or implicitly made, are worth reiterating in conclusion:

(1) The Gospels, like the books of the Bible generally, are church documents, composed out of church tradition, in and for the early Christian churches. While this certainly does not mean that the Gospels can be understood only by church people, it does imply that they may be at home in a church milieu today.

(2) The evangelists and their antecedents were in a broader sense Christian preachers, that is, heralds of the good news. The contemporary preacher can profit from an awareness of the possibility of continuing this homiletical tradition. For example, Mark as a preacher permits and even enlists present-day counterparts.

(3) Contemporary Christian preaching on the basis of the Gospels naturally and appropriately begins with the question of what those ancient writers intended to convey to their churches. That historical meaning does not necessarily prescribe the sermon, although it may proscribe certain sermons. To ask what meaning a text would have had in antiquity is a good and, in the Christian tradition, necessary preparation for asking what it may mean today.

(4) There is no one contemporary meaning or application of a Gospel text. The interpreter tries to grasp the intent, bearing, or thrust of a text. What is the author doing with his tradition? In this way continuity with the evangelist and his church, and even with Jesus and his disciples, is established. While the Gospel does not convey the history of Jesus pure and simple, it nevertheless brings the reader or hearer into meaningful contact with that history.

(5) The method ingredient, central, and essential to this whole enterprise is exegesis, the process of discerning as accurately as possible what the text is and what it intended to say, and to what effect. Exegesis,

properly practiced, does not stultify the imagination, whether historical, theological, or homiletical, but directs it and limits it.

(6) Exegesis does not quench the Spirit either; properly practiced, it
enables the preacher to "test the spirits to see whether they are of God"
(1 John 4:1). Exegesis is at the service of the Gospel text. As a hermeneutical process it guards against a subjective or capricious reading
of texts.

(7) As a general rule, in exegesis for preaching one should proceed on
the basis of a text (or texts) chosen from a single Gospel. Although not
inviolable, a good rule of thumb is not to mix texts from the different Gospels. (At times, of course, the interpretation of one text may
be advanced by a comparison with its parallels.) In particular, the
preacher should not combine synoptic and Johannine texts or material
indiscriminately.

Exegesis as historically informed interpretation is not all of preaching, and it cannot by itself guarantee authentic preaching. Yet exegesis
can and should play a significant, and for our time indispensable, role in
bringing such preaching forth. This is particularly true of exegesis of
the Gospels.

NOTES

CHAPTER 1

1. Albert Schweitzer, *The Quest of the Historical Jesus: A Critical Study of Its Progress from Reimarus to Wrede*, trans. W. Montgomery with a new introduction by James M. Robinson (New York: Macmillan Publishing Co., 1968 [E.T.:1910]).

2. See E. Hennecke, *New Testament Apocrypha*, vol. 2, *Writings Relating to the Apostles, Apocalypses, and Related Subjects*, ed. W. Schneemelcher, trans. R. McL. Wilson (Philadelphia: Westminster Press, 1965), pp. 333, 354. The description is from the Acts of Paul 3:3.

3. T. R. Glover, *The Jesus of History* (New York: Association Press, 1917), pp. 12, 16. Glover does not hesitate to infer from the Gospels the thoughts, experiences, and feelings of Jesus that presumably lay behind them. There are discussions of Jesus' habits of thought (pp. 51–55), his personality and genius for friendship (pp. 73–77), his understanding of the cross (pp. 166–68), and his God-consciousness (pp. 89–113). Although Glover's first canon of historical criticism is "to give the man's words his own meaning" (p. 18), he also insists that Jesus, like all great personages, breaks through the bonds of the customary ways of thought of his own period. Thus, the true Jesus is not the antiquarian's Jesus—and the historian allows ample latitude for interpretation.

4. Ibid., pp. 72–73.

5. *Best Sermons, 1964*, vol. 9, Protestant Edition, ed. G. Paul Butler (Princeton: D. Van Nostrand Co., 1964), p. 36.

6. Ibid., pp. 50–51.

7. See Glover, *The Jesus of History*, pp. 167–69.

8. Billy Graham, *The Secret of Happiness: Jesus' Teaching on Happiness as Expressed in the Beatitudes* (Garden City, N.Y.: Doubleday & Co., 1955).

9. Ibid., pp. 7–17.

10. Ibid., p. 6. Only the reference to Jesus' sitting and the last brief sentence are based on anything in the text (cf. Matt. 5:2).

CHAPTER 2

1. Martin Dibelius, *From Tradition to Gospel*, trans. Bertram Lee Woolf (New York: Charles Scribner's Sons, 1935).

2. Rudolf Bultmann, *The History of the Synoptic Tradition*, trans. John Marsh (New York: Harper & Row, 1963). The 1968 revision of the original translation should, however, be consulted.

3. For an evaluation of the impact of Schweitzer with extensive citation of relevant literature, see James M. Robinson's introduction to the 1968 English

edition (see above, chapter 1, note 1). For the history of modern discussion of the concept of the kingdom of God in Jesus' teaching, see Norman Perrin, *The Kingdom of God in the Teaching of Jesus* (Philadelphia: Westminster Press, 1963), esp. pp. 28–36, an excellent exposition of Schweitzer's position. The entire work is devoted to the questions Schweitzer and Johannes Weiss put before New Testament scholarship. Without denying the roots of Jesus' concept of the kingdom of God in Jewish apocalyptic, Perrin later endeavored to explore its symbolic nature and depth. See his *Jesus and the Language of the Kingdom: Symbol and Metaphor in New Testament Interpretation* (Philadelphia: Fortress Press, 1976). It is probably fair to say that Schweitzer's attempt to interpret the Gospel as history by using Jesus' kingdom expectation as the key to the continuity of the narrative has come to grief on the insights and perspectives of form and tradition criticism (of which we shall yet have more to say). His treatment of Jesus' concept of the kingdom as entirely future, with its resulting "interim ethics," has been resisted on the grounds that it ignores the New Testament evidence according to which the kingdom is in some sense present or dawning. Moreover, it represents as a warrant for Jesus' hard sayings (turning the other cheek, going the extra mile) the urgency and brevity of the period before the kingdom, a factor Jesus himself seldom, if ever, directly adduces in support of his injunctions.

4. Leander E. Keck, *The Bible in the Pulpit: The Renewal of Biblical Preaching* (Nashville: Abingdon Press, 1978), pp. 22–30.

5. Cf. Charles H. Talbert, *What Is a Gospel? The Genre of the Canonical Gospels* (Philadelphia: Fortress Press, 1977).

6. Dibelius, *From Tradition to Gospel*, p. 13.

7. Ibid., p. 15.

8. C. H. Dodd, *The Apostolic Preaching and Its Developments* (New York: Harper & Brothers, 1936), p. 47.

9. Rudolf Bultmann, "A New Approach to the Synoptic Problem," in *Existence and Faith: Shorter Writings of Rudolf Bultmann*, ed. Schubert M. Ogden (New York: Meridian Books, 1960), p. 38. The essay originally appeared in *The Journal of Religion* 6 (1926): 337–62.

10. Rudolf Bultmann, *Jesus and the Word*, trans. Louise Pettibone Smith and Erminie Huntress Lantero (New York: Charles Scribner's Sons, 1934).

11. I cite from memory. Knox gave this account during his Grey Lectures at Duke University, but it apparently was not incorporated in *The Integrity of Preaching* (Nashville: Abingdon Press, 1957), which is based on those lectures.

12. Joachim Jeremias, *The Parables of Jesus*, rev. ed., trans. S. H. Hooke (New York: Charles Scribner's Sons, 1963).

13. Although I have seen the film, these and subsequent comments have been checked against William Barclay, *Jesus of Nazareth* (London and Cleveland: Collins, Williams & World Publishing Co., 1977), a volume described as "based on the film directed by Franco Zeffirelli from the script by Anthony Burgess, Suso Cecchi d'Amico and Franco Zeffirelli."

14. For excellent, informative discussions of the history, uses, and possible abuses of lectionaries, see the articles by John Reumann, Gerard S. Sloyan, Lloyd R. Bailey, Elizabeth Achtemeier, and Roy A. Harrisville in *Interpretation* 31 (April 1977) and the extensive literature referred to there.

CHAPTER 3

1. Birger Gerhardsson, *Memory and Manuscript: Oral Tradition and Written Transmission in Rabbinic Judaism and Early Christianity,* trans. Eric J. Sharpe, Acta Seminarii Neotestamentici Upsaliensis 22 (Uppsala, 1961). Cf. W. D. Davies's appreciative but critical review in "Reflections on a Scandinavian Approach to 'The Gospel Tradition,'" in *The Setting of the Sermon on the Mount* (Cambridge: Cambridge University Press, 1963), pp. 464–80. Gerhardsson has now reiterated his position and made it easily accessible to the English reader in *The Origins of the Gospel Traditions* (Philadelphia: Fortress Press, 1979).

2. Gerd Theissen, *Sociology of Early Palestinian Christianity,* trans. John Bowden (Philadelphia: Fortress Press, 1978).

3. *Divino Afflante Spiritu,* 33–34, as given in *Rome and the Study of Scripture: A Collection of Papal Enactments of the Study of Holy Scripture Together with the Decisions of the Biblical Commission,* 5th rev. and enlarged ed. (Indiana: St. Meinrad, 1953), pp. 96–97.

4. Willi Marxsen, *Mark the Evangelist: Studies on the Redaction History of the Gospel,* trans. James Boyce, Donald Juel, and William Poehlmann, with Roy A. Harrisville (Nashville: Abingdon Press, 1969), pp. 23–24.

5. Hans Conzelmann, *The Theology of St. Luke,* trans. Geoffrey Buswell (New York: Harper & Row, 1960), p. 9.

CHAPTER 4

1. *Gospel Parallels: A Synopsis of the First Three Gospels,* ed. Burton H. Throckmorton, Jr., 2d ed., rev. (New York: Thomas Nelson, 1957), pp. 88–90.

2. Kurt Aland, *Synopsis Quattuor Evangeliorum,* 9th ed. (Stuttgart: Württembergische Bibelanstalt, 1976), pp. 229–36.

3. Vincent Taylor, *The Formation of the Gospel Tradition,* 2d ed. (London: Macmillan & Co., 1935), pp. 149–50; Dibelius, *From Tradition to Gospel,* pp. 44, 115; Bultmann, *The History of the Synoptic Tradition,* p. 257.

4. Cf. Milan Machoveč, *A Marxist Looks at Jesus,* with an introduction by Peter Hebblethwaite (Philadelphia: Fortress Press, 1976), p. 128. Machoveč thinks Jesus' messianic consciousness arose out of a dialogue with Peter and other disciples about his role; the dialogue is represented in compressed form in the confession at Caesarea Philippi.

5. These levels are to be distinguished from, although they are not unrelated to, the three historical settings mentioned above (ch. 2). Those are the levels through which the materials of the Gospels presumably passed. The levels described here are the ones at which the narrative may be said to function.

CHAPTER 5
1. Preached in Duke University Chapel, July 9, 1978.
2. The parts of the sermon (introduction, transition, exegesis, etc.) are indicated in the text. When I write a sermon I habitually label the parts to remind myself where I have been and where I am going. I forgot to remove those labels before giving the manuscript to the chapel secretary who retyped it for reproduction and distribution on campus, but they serve a purpose here by allowing the structure of the sermon to be readily apparent.
3. A point rightly discerned and emphasized by Jack Dean Kingsbury, *Matthew: Structure, Christology, Kingdom* (Philadelphia: Fortress Press, 1975), and idem, *Matthew*, Proclamation Commentaries (Philadelphia: Fortress Press, 1977).

CHAPTER 6
1. The standard work on the infancy narratives is now Raymond E. Brown's magisterial *The Birth of the Messiah: A Commentary on the Infancy Narratives in Matthew and Luke* (Garden City, N.Y.: Doubleday & Co., 1977).
2. This was also the position of Martin Dibelius, "Jungfrauensohn und Krippenkind: Untersuchungen zur Geburtsgeschichte Jesu' im Lukas-Evangelium," *Botschaft und Geschichte: Gesammelte Aufsätze* (Tübingen: Mohr, 1953), 1:1–78 (first published 1932); see esp. pp. 9–17.
3. See Vincent Taylor, *The Historical Evidence for the Virgin Birth* (Oxford: Clarendon Press, 1920), esp. pp. 34–45; Taylor regards only Luke 1:34–35 as secondary. Bultmann, *The History of the Synoptic Tradition*, pp. 295–96, takes 1:34–37 to be secondary. The latter seems the sounder proposal, since verses 36–37 presuppose the startling announcement of verses 34–35. Dibelius, "Jungfrauensohn," pp. 16–17, rejects all efforts to excise 1:34–37 as secondary.
4. Preached in Duke University Chapel, December 1, 1974. Luke 1:26–38 is not, of course, the Gospel reading for the First Sunday in Advent, when this sermon was actually preached. (It is the Gospel for the Fourth Sunday of Advent of Year B in the ecumenical lectionaries.) Because I was preparing an expository article on this text, an article which appeared in *Interpretation* 29 (1975): 411–17, I was allowed to preach from it on that occasion.
5. Cf. Raymond E. Brown, "The Problem of the Virginal Conception of Jesus," *Theological Studies* 33 (1972): 3–34, esp. p. 16.

CHAPTER 8
1. See J. Louis Martyn, *History and Theology in the Fourth Gospel*, rev. ed. (Nashville: Abingdon Press, 1979), pp. 66–67, 70–73, 79–81, for the view that such passages as John 5:18 (cf. 7:19; 8:59; 10:31) indicate that Christian believers in the synagogue were in danger of legal processes possibly culminating in execution. (Martyn has convincingly argued that the Fourth Gospel testifies to conflict between Jews and Christians and the expulsion of the latter from synagogues.) But Douglas R. A. Hare, *The Theme of Jewish Persecution of*

Christians in the Gospel according to Matthew, Society for New Testament Studies Monograph Series 6 (Cambridge: Cambridge University Press, 1967), pp. 20–43, examines the New Testament and other early evidence and concludes that while a few Christians, such as Stephen, were undoubtedly killed by Jews, their deaths were the result of mob action, that is, lynching, rather than judicial process. He observes that in the later New Testament books (1 Timothy to Revelation) and in the apostolic fathers there are no reported instances of Christians being put to death by Jews (p. 43, n. 1). In undeniable cases, the difference of opinion is over the question of the legal, or extralegal, character of instances in which Christians were killed by Jewish antagonists. That such actions justify modern antisemitism, persecution, or pogroms is on specifically Christian terms unthinkable.

2. The underlying social basis for the theological conceptuality or ideology of John is explored by Wayne A. Meeks in a pioneering article, "The Man from Heaven in Johannine Sectarianism," *Journal of Biblical Literature* 91 (1972): 44–72.

3. On the meaning of the term, one should consult the standard lexical work of Walter Bauer, *A Greek-English Lexicon of the New Testament and Other Early Christian Literature,* trans. W. F. Arndt and F. W. Gingrich, revised and augmented by F. W. Gingrich and F. W. Danker, 2d ed. (Chicago: University of Chicago Press, 1979), as well as the article *"Parakletos"* by J. Behm in *Theological Dictionary of the New Testament,* ed. Gerhard Kittel, trans. and ed. Geoffrey W. Bromiley, 9 vols. (Grand Rapids, Mich.: Wm. B. Eerdmans Publishing Co., 1964–76), 5:800–814.

4. The close relationship between the Paraclete and Jesus has been emphasized by Raymond E. Brown, "The Paraclete in the Fourth Gospel," *New Testament Studies* 13 (1967): 113–32.

5. Cf. G. Johnston, *The Spirit-Paraclete in the Gospel of John,* Society for New Testament Studies Monograph Series 12 (Cambridge: Cambridge University Press, 1970). Johnston links the Gospel and the evangelist with such Spirit-inspired prophecy (pp. 119, 126).

6. See William Wrede, *The Messianic Secret,* trans. J. C. G. Greig (Cambridge: James Clarke, 1971), pp. 181–210, esp. p. 186: "We can accordingly be in no doubt about John's having a view closely related to that of Mark in regard to the disciples' recognition of Jesus. In this it is of value to note that he expressly singles out the resurrection as the decisive moment in time." Cf. also pp. 204–7.

BIBLIOGRAPHY

The following brief bibliography consists only of commentaries in English which reflect recent trends in Gospel criticism. Even within these limits it is not comprehensive. Older commentaries may be valuable for historical and philological detail, but as a rule they will not afford adequate perspective for interpretation. A more extensive bibliography in English is available in the Proclamation Commentaries cited below. Also very useful for preaching are the related books published regularly under the title *Proclamation: Aids for Interpreting the Lessons of the Church Year* (Philadelphia: Fortress Press, 1973–76). See also *Proclamation 2: Aids for Interpreting the Lessons of the Church Year,* ed. Elizabeth Achtemeier, Gerhard Krodel, Charles P. Price (Philadelphia: Fortress Press, 1979–   ). Exactly what the name implies, the Proclamation Aids are written by distinguished biblical scholars with a view to helping the preacher interpret the lectionary text. In the same connection, the substantial work of Reginald H. Fuller, *Preaching the New Lectionary: The Word of God for the Church Today* (Collegeville, Minn.: Liturgical Press, 1975), as well as Gerard S. Sloyan, *Commentary on the New Lectionary* (New York: Paulist Press, 1975), is quite useful. All the commentaries noted are deemed useful and recommended; only qualifications are noted.

MARK

Achtemeier, Paul J. *Mark.* Proclamation Commentaries. Philadelphia: Fortress Press, 1977. Like others in the series, not a commentary in the strict sense of the word but useful in providing insights and overall perspectives for interpretation by drawing upon the best recent scholarship.

Anderson, Hugh. *The Gospel of Mark.* New Century Bible. London: Oliphants, 1976.

Lane, William L. *The Gospel according to Mark: The English Text with Introduction, Exposition and Notes.* The New International Commentary on the New Testament. Grand Rapids, Mich.: Wm. B. Eerdmans Publishing Co., 1974. Conservative, compendious, well-informed.

Schweizer, Eduard. *The Good News according to Mark.* Translated by Donald H. Madvig. Atlanta: John Knox Press, 1970.

Taylor, Vincent. *The Gospel according to St. Mark: The Greek Text with Introduction, Notes, and Indexes*. 2d ed. London: Macmillan & Co., 1966. Still the standard commentary on the Greek text in English. Taylor is knowledgeable about form criticism, although somewhat conservative, but he wrote before the development of the discipline of redaction criticism.

MATTHEW

Hill, David. *The Gospel of Matthew*. New Century Bible. London: Oliphants, 1972.

Kingsbury, Jack Dean. *Matthew*. Proclamation Commentaries. Philadelphia: Fortress Press, 1977.

McNeile, Alan Hugh. *The Gospel according to St. Matthew: The Greek Text with Introduction, Notes, and Indices*. London: Macmillan & Co., 1915. Relatively old, but still the most recent commentary in English on the Greek text.

Schweizer, Eduard. *The Good News according to Matthew*. Translated by David E. Green. Atlanta: John Knox Press, 1975.

LUKE

Creed, John Martin. *The Gospel according to St. Luke: The Greek Text with Introduction, Notes, and Indices*. London: Macmillan & Co., 1930. Like other synoptic commentaries on the Greek text, this one needs to be brought up-to-date. Nevertheless, it remains a useful tool.

Danker, Frederick W. *Luke*. Proclamation Commentaries. Philadelphia: Fortress Press, 1976.

Ellis, E. Earle. *The Gospel of Luke*. New Century Bible. London: Nelson, 1967.

Marshall, I. Howard. *The Gospel of Luke: A Commentary on the Greek Text*. The New International Greek Testament Commentary. Exeter, Eng.: Paternoster, 1978.

JOHN

Barrett, C. K. *The Gospel according to St. John: An Introduction with Commentary and Notes on the Greek Text*. 2d rev. ed. Philadelphia: Westminster Press, 1978.

Brown, Raymond E. *The Gospel according to John: Introduction, Translation, and Notes*. 2 vols. The Anchor Bible 29, 29A. Garden City, N.Y.: Doubleday & Co., 1966, 1970.

Bultmann, Rudolf. *The Gospel of John: A Commentary*. Translated by G. R. Beasley-Murray with R. W. N. Hoare and J. K. Riches. Philadelphia: Westminster Press, 1971. Basically the commentary that was published nearly forty years ago in German, but still a classic.

Lindars, Barnabas. *The Gospel of John*. New Century Bible. London: Oliphants, 1972.

Smith, D. Moody. *John*. Proclamation Commentaries. Philadelphia: Fortress Press, 1976.

INDEXES

SCRIPTURE REFERENCES

Genesis
16:11—67
18:9–15—67

Judges
5:24—67
13:2–7—67
13:3—67

2 Samuel
7:12–16—66

Isaiah
[6:9–10]—58
6:9–10—63
7:14—67

Zechariah
13:7—90

Matthew
1:18–25—67
[5:1, 2]—12
[5:3]—11–12
5:17—26
7:24–29—63
[9:9]—10
10:38–39—49
13:1–23—55–65
[13:10–15]—58
13:13—63
13:19—59
13:23—59
13:51—59, 65
16:13–20—48
16:17–19—48
22:1–10—25
23—100
28:16–20—63

Mark
1:14–15—17
1:21–45—23
2:1–3:6—23
2:27–28—25
3:2—25
3:6—25
4—23
[4:10–12]—58
4:13—63
4:34—63
4:35–41—20–21
5—23
6—23
6:1–6—23
7—23
7:1–23—35
8—23
8–10—23, 91
8:22—37
8:22–26—35
8:22–10:52—35–38
8:27—46
8:27–30—35, 46, 48
8:27–33—46
8:27–35—46
8:27–38—46
8:27–9:1—45–54
8:30—50
8:31—35, 47, 49, 50
8:31–33—46
8:31–38—35
8:32—49, 50
8:32a—47
8:34–36—47, 49
8:34–91—46
8:34ff.—50
8:35–37—47
8:38—47 49

9:1—47, 50
9:2—46
9:2–8—35
9:9–10—49
9:31—35, 49
9:32—49
9:33–37—35
9:33ff.—49
10:17–22—10
10:33—49
10:33–34—35
10:34—49
10:35–45—35
10:35ff.—49
10:43–45—36
11:1–11—36
12—23
12:13–17—92
13—23
13:23—62
14:27—90
14:50—90

Luke
1:1—23
1:18–24—68
1:26–38—66–75, 108
1:28—67
1:31—67
[1:31–38]—72
1:32–33—66
1:34–35—67, 108
1:34–37—67, 108
1:36–37—108
1:68—75
2:34–35—75
[4:16–30]—23
12:9—49
14:15–24—25

14:27—49
24:21—75
24:34—48

John
2—97
2:11—90
2:17—85, 88
2:22—85, 88
3:16—88
3:17-19—91
5:18—108
5:19—89
7:19—108
7:33-34—89
7:39—85, 86
8:21—89
8:23—92
8:59—108
9—93, 100
9:22—83, 84
10:31—108
12:16—85, 88
12:31-32—91
12:35—89
12:42—83, 84
13:1—88
13:33—89
13:34-35—88
14—86
14:5ff—90
14:5—86
14:15-17—88
14:16—86
14:18—89
14:19—89
14:22—89

14:25-26—88
14:26—86, 88
14:27—91
14-16—83
15:18—83
15:18-19—85
15:26—86
15:25-26—88
15:26-27—88
15-16—83, 86
16—83-94, 96, 97
16:1—85
16:1-4—83, 93
16:2—83, 84
16:2-3—85
16:3—85
16:4—85
16:5—86
16:7—86, 90
16:8-11—86, 91
16:12-13—87
16:12-15—87, 88
16:13—86, 87
16:15—88
16:16—89
16:16-24—89, 90
16:17-18—89
16:19—89
16:19ff.—89
16:20—89
16:23—89
16:25—90
16:26-27—89
16:28—89, 90
16:29-30—90
16:31-32—90
16:33—91, 93

17—86
17:8—89
17:14—83
17:15—91
19:15—85
20:22—86
20:26-29—91
20:30-31—22
21—93
21:25—22

Acts
1:6—75
28:23-28—75

Romans
1:17—3
2:29—84

1 Corinthians
11:23—15
15:5—48

2 Corinthians
4:5—27
12:8-9—87

1 Thessalonians
5:21—87

1 John
2:1—86
4:1—87
4:1-3—87

Revelation
1-3—87

MODERN AUTHORS AND SCHOLARS

Achtemeier, Elizabeth, 107, 111
Achtemeier, Paul J., 111
Aland, Kurt, 46, 107
Anderson, Hugh, 111

Arndt, W. F., 109

Bailey, Lloyd R., 107
Barclay, William, 106

Barrett, C. K., 112
Bauer, Walter, 109
Beasley-Murray, G. R., 112
Behm, J. 109
Boyce, James 107
Bromiley, Geoffrey W., 109
Brown, Raymond E., 70, 98, 108, 109, 112
Bultmann, Rudolf, 15–17, 19, 20, 29, 31, 48, 51, 67, 105–8, 112
Burgess, Anthony, 106
Buswell, Geoffrey, 107
Butler, G. Paul, 105

Cecchi d'Amico, Suso, 106
Cleland, James T., ix, 16, 56
Conzelmann, Hans, 33, 107
Creed, John Martin, 112
Cushman, Robert E., 16

Danker, Frederick W., 109, 112
Davies, W. D., 16, 29, 107
Dibelius, Martin, 15–16, 18–19, 29, 31, 48, 74, 100, 105–8
Dodd, C. H., 16, 18–19, 98, 106

Ellis, E. Earle, 112

Fuller, Reginald H., 111

Gerhardsson, Birger, 29–30, 107
Gingrich, F. W., 109
Glover, T. R., x, 8–13, 105
Graham, Billy, x, 11–12, 105
Green, David E., 112
Greig, J. E. G., 109

Hare, Douglas R. A., 108
Harrisville, Roy A., 107
Hebblethwaite, Peter, 107
Hennecke, E., 105
Hill, David, 112
Hoare, R. W. N., 112

Jeremias, Joachim, 24–25, 62, 106
Johnston, G., 109

Keck, Leander, 18, 106
Kingsbury, Jack Dean, 108, 112

Kittel, Gerhard, 109
Knox, John, 20–21, 106
Krodel, Gerhard, 111

Lane, William L., 111
Lindars, Barnabas, 112
Lischer, Richard, x

McCowen, Alec, 100–101
Machoveč, Milan, 107
McNeile, Alan Hugh, 112
Marshall, I. Howard, 112
Martyn, J. Louis, 108
Marxsen, Willi, 33, 107
Meeks, Wayne A., 109
Montgomery, W., 105

Pasolini, 100
Perrin, Norman, 106
Pius XII, pope, 32
Poehlmann, William, 107
Price, Charles P., 111

Reumann, John, 107
Robinson, James M., 105

Schmidt, K. L., 20
Schneemelcher, W., 105
Schweitzer, Albert, 4, 8–13, 16, 17, 20, 105–6
Schweizer, Eduard, 111–12
Sharpe, Eric J., 107
Sloyan, Gerard S., 107, 111
Smith, D. Moody, 112

Talbert, Charles H., 106
Taylor, Vincent, 48, 67, 107–8, 112
Theissen, Gerd, 30, 107
Throckmorton, Burton H., Jr., 107

Weiss, Johannes, 20, 106
Wellhausen, J., 19
Willimon, William H., x
Wilson, R. McL., 105
Wrede, William, 20, 109

Young, Franklin W., x

Zeffirelli, Franco, 26, 99, 106

SUBJECTS

Annunciation, the, 66–75

Beatitudes, the, 11–12
Bible
    character of, 3–4
    and church, 3–6
    interpretation, 4–6
Biography, and the Gospels, 8–9,
    18–19

Canon, Gospels in, 7, 98–99
Commentaries, 111–12
Context
    of Gospel pericopes, 26–28
    in John, 92–93

Didache, the, 79
Discipleship, in Mark, 37–39,
    51–53
Divino Afflante Spiritu, 32–33

Exegesis, 103–4
    as contrasted with eisegesis,
        10–11
    as defined in Divino Afflante
        Spiritu, 32
    of the Fouth Gospel, 79
    of the parable of the sower, 57–59
    particularly useful commentaries,
        111–12
    relation to exposition and
        application, 56
    relation to preaching, 30–31,
        61–62, 72–73, 75

Farewell Discourses (of the Gospel
    of John), 83–94
Form criticism, ix, 15–27, 29–31,
    32
    of the Lucan birth narratives, 74
    of the parable of the sower, 62

Gabriel, the angel, 67, 68–69, 72, 74
Gospels
    character of, 103
    chronology (see Ordering of
        gospel material, principles
        of)

and gospel message (kerygma), 7
as history or historical writing, 7,
    8–11
and Jesus (see Jesus: and Gospels)
as texts for preaching, 95–96,
    98–99, 101, 104
tradition (see Form criticism)

History and interpretation
    in the Gospel of John, 81–82
    in relation to the Lucan birth
        narratives, 73–74
Holy Spirit, 67, 72
    described as Paraclete in John,
        86–89

Ignatius, letters of, 79

Jesus, 4–13
    apocalyptic view, 11
    departure and return in John,
        86–87
    eschatology, 11–12, 17–18, 25,
        106
    experiences and feelings, 105
    and Gospels, 5–11
    as historical problem, 8–9, 16,
        53–54, 79–82
    and Marcan redaction, 40–41
    Mary's son, 67, 68–70, 72, 74–75
    messiahship in Mark, 35–38
    messianic consciousness, 107
    as portrayed in the Gospel of
        John, 79–82
    outside the Gospels, 6–7
    relationship to disciples, 9–10
    relationship to parable of the
        sower, 64–65
    virgin birth of, 66–75
"The Jews," as opponents of Jesus
    in John, 83–85
Johannine Christianity, 81, 83
John the Baptist, 67–68, 74
John, Gospel of, 7, 24, 79–101
    commentaries, 112
    conflict with Judaism, 93–94,
        108–9
    historical value, 79–81

literary contexts, 92–93
portrayal of Jesus, 79–82
postresurrection perspective, 85–86, 89–91
prologue, 93
sermonic character, 91–92, 94
and the Synoptics, 79–80, 83, 96–99, 101
Joseph, 67, 68–70, 74

Kerygma, Gospels as, 18–19
Kingdom of God, 11, 106 (See also Jesus: eschatology, apocalyptic view)
and parables, 25, 27

Lectionaries, 28, 46, 107
use in delimiting pericopes, 27–28
L-source, 63, 79
Luke, Gospel of, 66–75
commentaries, 112
relation to Mark, ix, 23, 34, 55–56, 96
relation to Matthew, 96
in birth narratives, 67–69, 74
theological view of history, 72, 74–75
work of a historian, 67

McCowen's St. Mark's Gospel, 100–101
Marcan hypothesis, ix
Mark, Gospel of, 35–41, 45–54
audience of, 37–41, 51–54
commentaries, 111–12
and the contemporary preacher, 51–54
disciples' misunderstanding, 36, 49, 63–64; cf. 37–39, 51–52
importance of messianic question for, 80
as kerygma, 19
McCowen's recitation, 100–101
redaction of, 49–50
relation to Luke, ix, 23, 34, 55–56, 96
relation to Matthew, ix, 23, 34, 55–56, 96
structuring of, 23–24, 25–26

Mary, mother of Jesus, 67, 68–70, 72, 74–75
Matthew, Gospel of, 55–65
commentaries, 112
Pasolini's film, 100
Peter's confession, 48, 51, 53
relation to Luke, 96
relation to Luke in birth narratives, 67–69, 74
relation to Mark, ix, 23, 34, 55–56, 96
theme of understanding, 63–65
Messiahship of Jesus, as a theme in Mark, 37–38, 50–53
Miracle, the miraculous
in the Lucan birth narrative, 66, 68, 68–71, 72–74
in Mark, 36–38, 40
Misunderstanding of disciples, in John, 90–91
M-source, 63, 79

Narratives, character of gospel, 21–24

Old Testament, in Lucan birth narrative, 66–68, 72, 74–75
Ordering of gospel material, principles of, 23–27

Papias, 24
Parable of the sower
in Mark, 55, 58–59, 64
in Matthew, 55–65
Parables
and kingdom of God, 27
original form and context, 24–25
Paraclete, 86–90, 109. See also Holy Spirit
relation of Jesus to, 86–89
Parousia of Jesus, in John, 89–90
Pasolini's The Gospel according to St. Matthew, 100
Paul, apostle, 6
Peter's confession, 28, 45–54
historical question, 48–51
Matthean version, 48, 51, 53
in pre-Gospel tradition, 52–53
Pharisees, in the Gospels, 23, 25–26
Plato, 9

Preaching
    gospels as, 20–21 (see also
        Kerygma)
    and New Testament scholarship,
        30–31

Q-source, 63, 79

Redaction criticism, ix, 30–41
    analysis of text, 34–35
    evangelist's situation, 33–38
    and historicity, 33
    of Lucan birth narrative, 67–68,
        74–75
    of parable of the sower, 58–59,
        62–63
    structural considerations, 35–36
Resurrection of Jesus, in John,
    89–91
Revelation, Book of, possible
    relation to Fourth Gospel, 87
Revelation, concept of, in Fourth
    Gospel, 87–88 (see also
    Paraclete)
Romans, Paul's Epistle to, 7

Sallman's Head of Christ, 6
Secrecy, of Jesus in Mark, 46–47
Sermons (on Gospel texts), 56–61,
    68–72

Socrates, 9
Synagogue, expulsion of Christians
    in John, 83–85
Synoptic Gospels and John. See
    John, Gospel of, and synoptics

Temple cleansing, in John and
    Synoptics, 97–98
Thomas, doubting, 93
Thomas, Gospel of, 59, 79
Tradition
    in narratives of Jesus' Birth,
        67–68, 74
    separation from redaction of
        Mark, 48–51

Virgin birth of Jesus, 66–75
    influence of Greco-Roman world,
        66, 74
    influence of Old Testament on
        Lucan narrative, 66–67, 72,
        74–75

World, hostility of, in the Gospel of
    John, 83–85

Zechariah, father of John the
    Baptist, 67–68, 74–75
Zeffirelli's Jesus of Nazareth, 26,
    99–100